Talleur's

DRY-FLY
HANDBOOK

Talleur's

DRY-FLY
HANDBOOK

DICK TALLEUR

Lyons & Burford, Publishers

Printed in the United States of America

10 9 8 7 6 5 4 3 2 1

Library of Congress Cataloging-in-Publication Data

Talleur, Richard W.
[Dry-fly handbook]
Talleur's dry-fly handbook / Dick Talleur.
p.   cm.
Includes bibliographical references (p.   ) and index.
ISBN 1-55821-159-4
1. Trout fishing—Handbooks, manuals, etc.   2. Fly fishing—
Handbooks, manuals, etc.   I. Title.
SH687.T27   1992
799.1'755—dc20   91-40220
CIP

The photographs in this book were taken
by Matt Vinciguerra, Kimberly Vigars, and the author.
The illustrations are by Linda Peterson.

To all of those anglers and anglerettes
who like it on top.

CONTENTS

FOREWORD

This book is about fishing the dry fly, something I passionately love to do. In some situations, other forms of fly fishing are more effective than dry-fly fishing; however, many anglers, myself included, will stay with the floater when a subsurface fly might be taken more readily. It's a challenge of sorts, and a test of skill.

While I enjoy and am reasonably competent at all types of fly fishing, dry bug is my preference. I feel that I fish it more skillfully than I do, say, a weighted nymph, and thus, to a degree, compensate for the fact that the fish may prefer a fly presented beneath the surface. I wouldn't flail away with the dry in a hopeless situation when I could be catching fish on a sunken nymph or something, but given a reasonable chance for success, I'll be on top.

I've divided the book into two sections; the first addresses orientation, the second, on-stream techniques. In both, there's a great deal of information applicable to fly fishing in general. I've included it for completeness, so that the reader needn't constantly be bouncing back and forth between this and other references to get the picture. But please understand that the dissertations on equipment, leaders and what-have-you, and also the on-stream techniques are offered within the context of dry-flyfishing.

My publisher, Nick Lyons, and myself decided that black and white photos would suffice. Color is always attractive, but it adds considerably to the cost (and price) of a book. From a standpoint of form and function, we feel that black-and-white photos, plus some illustrations, will serve perfectly well.

On that note, I wish you the greatest of success in dry-fly fishing, and hope that you find my experiences to be of value.

Dick Talleur

PART ONE

ORIENTATION

DRY-FLY FISHING LOGICALLY DIVIDES INTO TWO MAJOR pieces: doing it and preparing for it. This brief dissertation introduces the latter.

All fly fishing involves technology of a sort. In my opinion, dry-fly fishing epitomizes this. It is a very precise game. So many aspects of it require strict attention to minute detail; casting, selection of tackle, leaders and knots, understanding stream insects, fly selection. These are the topics to be dealt with in the five chapters that comprise Part One.

Please understand that some of my recommendations are not absolute, but are intended to help the reader refine and optimize. For example, if you don't happen to own a nine-foot, five-weight graphite fly rod, but do happen to have a fiberglass eight-footer, rig it up and go fishing! Catch some trout, and enjoy yourself. Later, perhaps you'll want to try the nine-footer, and you'll find that it offers certain advantages, and you'll buy it. And maybe you'll fish the eight-foot fiberglass rod for the next quarter of a century and be perfectly happy.

Regardless of your choice of tackle, I strongly suggest that you become familiar with the information in these earlier chapters. Efficient casting is the key to all fly fishing, none more so than dry fly. Leaders make a world of difference, as do the knots used to connect them to the line and the fly. The selection of artificial flies offered today is overwhelming, and a functional understanding of them by type, or design, is most valuable. And it's important to develop an appreciation of the insect life that comprises the food you're trying to imitate, for without it, you'll have difficulty coping with the selectivity so often encountered when insects are on the water.

The competent, well-informed fly fisher makes his own decisions. Yes, there are some good people working in fly shops, and of course, an endless array of information, some helpful, much strictly sales promo. Would you base a decision for buying, let's say, a personal computer only on a T.V. ad, or what the salesman told you? Hardly! So don't make the same mistake regarding fly tackle.

I hope you will find my suggestions helpful, and will put them to use. I've been fly fishing since 1955, and I've learned a lot, mostly through trial and error. It is my wish that my experiences will not only enable you to fish more successfully and enjoyably, but will save you money and frustration as well.

With that, let's examine fly casting, from the dry-fly fisher's standpoint.

The Dry Fly

WHAT IS DRY FLY FISHING?

Dry-fly fishing encompasses any type of fly fishing in which the fly is presented on the surface. A wide variety of fish can be caught under this broad definition, but in this book I will concentrate on fishing for trout, with some additional information on surface fishing for Atlantic salmon.

Angling writers have, with few exceptions, represented dry-fly fishing to be the most difficult form, the apex of the sport. Conversely, I believe it's the easiest. Yes, it can be maddeningly difficult under certain conditions, but generally I find it easier to instruct beginning fly fishers in using the dry than in any of the subsurface methods.

I say this because the dry-fly angler can see everything: the fly, the line, the leader, the drift. The behavior of the fly can much more readily be monitored than can a wet fly, and appropriate corrections made. The reactions of the fish, positive, negative or neutral, can often be clearly seen. And by the way, a neutral or nonreaction may be considered both ways; the fish didn't take (negative), but neither did it spook (positive).

Much is made of the detached-drift technique in dry-fly presentation. It is true that a drag-free float is what's wanted most of the time, but there are exceptions to that, which we will explore. In any case, the first thing one must do is get the fly out onto the water by way of the fundamental element of presentation, the cast. Various maneuvers are then used to make corrections and compensate for what the currents are doing to the drift of the fly.

In order to cast a fly, a virtually weightless and more or less wind-resistant object, we require fly-fishing tackle, which differs fundamentally from spinning and bait-casting gear. Let's begin our education in dry-fly fishing with an appreciation of that difference. It is easier to understand tackle when one is aware of what it is supposed to do.

THE CAST

Bait and spin casting involve propelling objects that have sufficient weight to more than offset air resistance. It's like throwing a baseball, or better yet, a lacrosse ball, which involves the use of a stick. The stick is essentially an extension of the player's arm, as is a fishing rod.

In any type of casting, the rod has two functions: to provide increased leverage and to magnify the power of the caster's arm. The latter is a function of the rod's action. By simple definition, *action* refers to the power generated when a flexed rod unflexes. I will expand upon this in the section on fly tackle.

In fly casting, dry-fly casting in particular, there is little weight in the lure itself, certainly not enough to lend impetus to a cast. Something else has to provide impetus, and that something is the line. It's important to fully appreciate that point; we cast the line, and the fly and leader go along for the ride. Thus, the fly-rod cast is simply a matter of putting the line in motion in an effective and controlled manner.

I will not go into detail here in teaching the basic cast, but merely touch upon a few points that I feel are essential. There are several fine books and videotapes available that do a first-rate job in treating the subject. I particularly recommend *The Essence Of Casting* by Mel Krieger, Joan Wulff's *Fly Casting Techniques*, and *Fly Casting with Lefty Kreh*, each of which is available in book or tape. There are also two extensive and explicit chapters on casting in my own book, *Fly Fishing for Trout; A Guide for Beginners*.

I believe it is quite feasible to learn fly casting from books and tapes. One of the distinct advantages is that you are instructed by top-flight people who know whereof they speak, and have developed effective teaching methods. It is, of course, most helpful to have a "live" instructor, provided that person has a proper understanding of fly casting, and the patience and skill to teach it. As with golf and tennis, this is more uncommon than one might think.

What *will* be covered in the forthcoming chapters are the particular techniques that facilitate dry-fly presentation in a wide range of situations. Usually, one must make some alteration of the basic cast to compensate for winds, currents, casting room, obstructions and all manner of things. We shall also examine the various options in tackle-rods, lines, leaders and reels-with an eye toward how they interact, and how they can be matched and mismatched, all within the context of presenting the dry fly.

Let us briefly examine the basic cast. As the aforementioned references and/or your personal instructor will tell you, the fly cast is simply a matter of getting the line moving in the air. It is propelled backward and forward (the back cast and forward cast) with sufficient speed to counteract gravity. This is called *false casting*. The line should travel in smooth,

Most people use this sort of grip.

A few people find it easier to keep from "breaking" the wrist by using the finger-on-top grip.

unrolling loops. Essentially, the smaller, or tighter these loops, the more efficient the cast. When all is in order, the final forward cast is allowed to unroll completely, and the fly is delivered to its destination.

A few suggestions. On the back cast, employ a lifting motion, throwing the line rearward on a slightly upward trajectory, to allow for gravity. Use the forearm, not the wrist, which should remain firm. Don't jerk the line—be quick through the arc, but smooth. Finish the back cast move with the rod tip high; don't tip it over toward the ground (or water), or you will create a wide, uncontrolled, "open" loop, with a lot of line standing vertically in the air. Such a back cast is not only inefficient; it is, in effect, stillborn, for all momentum simply dies.

When about to execute the pick-up that begins the back cast, try to position yourself with the casting arm extended and the line straight out ahead of you, so that interaction between the rod and line commences immediately.

Lift with the arm, mainly the forearm, keeping the wrist firm.

Execute a very quick, short stroke in this area, still keeping the wrist firm, and lifting.

Complete the back cast in approximately this position. The tip of the rod should not be tipped toward the ground as it stops, as this will result in an open loop, with the line being thrown toward the ground.

Begin your forward cast just as the line is about to straighten behind you, but *while the line is still travelling rearward*; thus the dynamic of the cast is continued. Again, be quick and smooth, and don't tip the end of the rod over, or you will get that wide loop. On the delivery, extend your arm toward the target, aiming fairly high, so that the line has time to unfurl, straighten the leader and deliver the fly.

On the forward cast, another short, quick stroke is executed in this area.

Note that there is still no wrist action involved.

At this point in the forward cast, tip the thumb a bit, which brings the rod tip slightly downward, allowing the loop of line to pass above without tailing.

Finish with the rod level and fairly high, so that the cast can straighten above the water, and the fly drop into the target area.

Whatever you do, don't do this on the pick-up. . . .

Or this on the back cast.

An ideal place for a beginner to practice is on a pond or lake with plenty of unobstructed space to the rear, such as a beach. Lawns are fine, but parking lots and paved surfaces are not; they eat up fly lines in a hurry. A river or stream usually involves wading and may have strong currents, which will present problems to the beginner. Time enough for all that later on.

Always have a leader of some sort attached to the line when practicing, or it will crack like a buggywhip when the loop reverses. It's like having a tail on a kite. Also, tie a small bit of yarn at the tip of the leader to simulate a fly, or a junk fly with the hook bend cut off. This saves the leader tip from fraying, and closely approximates the true experience and feel of casting. The leader should be fairly short; eight feet is plenty for a beginner to use in rehearsal.

2

The Outfit

Fly Rods

Most modern fly rods are made of carbon-graphite fiber of some type, although there is still a little fiberglass around, and split cane, or bamboo, has made a resurgence with the affluent, the purists and the aesthetes. Designer-brand rods can be a bit pricey, but serviceable rods are well within the limits of the average budget. Some companies offer matched outfits—rod, reel and line-at a package price.

The two primary concerns in selecting a fly rod are action and length, and there is a definite relationship between the two, shorter rods generally being somewhat "faster." Such terms as fast, slow, medium, parabolic, semiparabolic and fast-tip are historically used to describe rod actions. They are somewhat imprecise, but are readily understood and still in vogue, so I will not undertake to change them.

All else being equal, the stiffer the rod, the faster the action, all else being equal. Stiffness is a product of both material and design, or *taper*. You will encounter advertisements where rod materials are referred to as having a particular "modulus"; high, low, or whatever. In this context, modulus means stiffness—an oversimplification, but close enough. This sort of terminology can be confusing to even experienced and knowledgeable fly fishers. Don't get hung up on it. Select your rods by how they feel and function, not by esoteric references.

Rods are classified by line weight, which means the weight of the fly line that optimally matches the rod's strength and action. For typical dry-fly fishing, fairly light outfits are appropriate. I do most of my fishing with four- and five-weights, and can effectively deliver practically any dry fly and leader.

There are trade offs in rod actions and lengths. Generally, I prefer a longer rod, now that advanced graphite has made it practical to build nine-foot rods that work with four- or five-weight lines. The long rod enables one to more effectively manage line on the water, rearranging loops and mending to correct for drag. Being a bit slower than their shorter, stiffer counterparts, these rods are also more gentle and forgiving, and less fish are apt to be broken off on the strike, especially when fine leader tippets are the order of the day. I also feel it is easier for a beginner to master casting with a long rod. The increased arc helps the imperfect caster generate line speed, the response of the rod is more readily felt, and timing is less critical.

On the negative side, a long rod can be an encumbrance in close cover, and is not the tool for fishing small, bush-bound streams. It can also be less than optimal for driving a cast into or under a wind, although experience will teach ways of compensating for this. It becomes a matter of matching the tackle to the fishing. Those who fish various and diverse types of water will want several outfits. I have a 6½ foot three-weight rod for coping with the confinements of small-stream fishing, an 8 foot, four-weight for windy days on western spring creeks and of course, my much-adored 9-footers.

But what of the beginner, the youngster, the casual angler, the person of limited means who can't afford or is not inclined to own an arsenal? For the one-rod dry-fly fisher, something in the order of an 8-foot four-weight or an 8½ foot five weight would be an excellent choice. These rods cast just about any dry fly, and serve yeoman duty on those unhappy occasions when the floater simply isn't the drill, and one must resort to the wet or nymph.

Let's further explore those rod-action terms mentioned earlier. *Fast*, *slow* and *medium* should be reasonably clear at this point. *Parabolic* refers to a rod that, when flexed, bends far down into the butt section and resembles the shape of a parabola. *Fast-tip* is just the opposite, with most of the action occurring in the tip section of the rod. *Semiparabolic* is a marriage of the two. Sometimes called *progressive action*, the term refers to a rod that flexes more in the upper portion, but also works well down into the butt section when loaded.

These terms represent rod-design choices that have a great deal to do with how the rod behaves. A true parabolic taper usually produces a fairly slow-action rod, although with modern graphite fiber that's not as absolute as it was in the era of cane and fiberglass. Fast-tip rods, which fortunately we don't see many of these days, were a compromise. Before graphite, the design was employed to make longer rods that would cast with a fairly light line. It didn't work very well, still doesn't, and with today's materials is no longer necessary.

A semiparabolic or progressive action is what we find in most contemporary fly rods. During the heyday of fiberglass, which encompassed the transition from silk to synthetic lines, variations of the progressive taper were used in an attempt to make rods less line-weight sensitive, and would cast with more than one specific weight. It was a poor compromise, because fiberglass simply wasn't strong enough. A light line got only the tip of the rod to respond (inefficient), while a heavier line developed action further down, but overburdened the tip. Graphite has solved all this.

If you can put off buying a rod until you've learned to cast fairly well, you'll be better prepared to make an informed choice. That's one of the benefits of the flyfishing schools and casting clinics that have sprung up in recent years; the students get to work out with loaned outfits. You might consider attending such a school, particularly if you find that casting doesn't come easily to you.

FLY LINES

In fly casting, the line is actually of greater importance than the rod. Consider that one could cast a fly with a spinning rod and a fly line, but could not do so with a fly rod and a spinning line. As stated earlier, it's the weight of the line that does the job.

Fly lines are rated by weight from number one (very light) to number thirteen (very heavy). Each category has a specification, measured in grains, for the first thirty feet of line. Slight variances, lighter or heavier, are allowed, to provide for minor inconsistencies in manufacturing. Occasionally, a few escape the watchful eye of the quality-control people, and some out-of-spec lines find their way into the hands of consumers. If you have been using a certain weight line with success and you replace it with another of the same weight and taper and it casts poorly, it could possibly be out of specification.

Lines are made either to float, or to sink at various rates. This being a dry-fly book, I will limit my discussion to the former. The modern plastic-coated floating fly line has an uncountable number of tiny bubbles (microballoons) trapped within the coating; these make the line buoyant. This buoyancy is rather marginal. Fly lines don't float high, like corks. They float in the surface film, like a green stick of wood. Heavier-weight lines are better floaters than lighter ones, because the greater amount of plastic coating accommodates more bubbles. In fact, the most annoying problem with the new ultralight lines, the one- and two-weights, is their poor floating properties.

The delicate balance between a line floating or not floating can be affected by several factors. Lines pick up minute amounts of slime and goo from the water, and that adversely affects the float. This is easily remedied by cleaning the line with a mild hand soap, such as Ivory. It is best to avoid harsh detergents, as they can be a bit rough on the line. Several very good commercial preparations are also available.

Lines can develop minute cracks, which will cause them to absorb water and sink, perhaps forever. Normal wear will eventually result in cracking, but it can be brought on prematurely by abuse. Don't stretch a fly line. If your fly gets caught up in a tree and moderate tension doesn't free it, try to devise some way to get it loose without exerting heavy strain on the line. Or break it off; lines are far more expensive than flies.

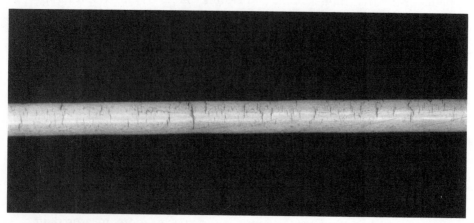

When a fly line develops cracks in the finish, its utility, at least for dry-fly fishing, is over.

Don't leave lines in places where bright sun will beat down on them, such as on the rear deck of an automobile; heat and light both have a deleterious effect. And it is advisable not to leave your reels with lines on them in cars or car trunks, because of heat buildup, but convenience generally wins in this case.

Beyond these cautions and an occasional washing, there's not much one needs to do by way of maintenance. There are coatings that can be applied that will make the line slide through the guides and shoot better; these are usually a form of vinyl polish, vinyl being the current compound of choice in fly-line manufacture. They work quite well, but will not restore a line that's over the hill.

It is important to realize that fly lines, as manufactured at this writing, have a shelf life, and quite a finite one at that. They will eventually self-destruct just by sitting, even in an optimal environment. The reason is a phenomenon called *plasticizing*. The compound that makes up the coating of the line is an imperfect mixture, a long-term emulsion that slowly degenerates, and the components separate. Once that happens, the line is done for. A notable figure in the fly tackle business recently told me he had created a substance that could reverse plasticizing if simply applied to a line. I suppose that's possible, and I hope it works; it wasn't yet available at this writing. If indeed it is effective, we will can expect a longer life for our lines, as plasticizing is the main culprit behind line degeneration.

Besides weight, the other major consideration when selecting a fly line is design, or *taper*. *Level*, or *untapered* lines are inexpensive but not very popular, as they do not have good aerodynamics, and therefore cast poorly. *Double-taper* lines are nicely suited to dry-fly work and have the advantage of being symmetrical, so that when one end becomes worn out, the line can be reversed. *Weight-forward*, or *forward-taper* lines have more weight up front and are efficient for both long and short casts. There are several variations of forward tapers from which to choose.

The dry-fly fisher may resort to a highly specialized type of line, the *shooting head*. This is composed of a relatively short section of weight-forward line followed by some light "shooting" line. The shooting line is deployed in loose coils on the water, the deck of a boat or perhaps in a stripping basket. The caster gets the head moving through the air at high speed, then lets it fly forward with considerable force. The shooting line goes along for the ride. Shooting heads can significantly increase the range of a caster. However, they are rather tricky to use and prone to tangles and other snafus. I recommend them only in extreme situations.

Fly Reels

If this were a dissertation on spinning or bait-casting, I would have begun with the reel, as it is the most critical of the three main components for those methods. In fly casting, the reverse is true; the reel is far less important and has very little to do with casting. It does, however, get involved in the actual fishing, sometimes quite significantly.

The fly reel's primary function is to serve as a receptacle for storing the line. It must have sufficient capacity to accommodate the thickness and length of line in question, along with an appropriate amount of backing. Backing is simply running line, and is very similar to braided bait-casting line. Dacron is favored for backing because it doesn't stretch very much, spooling neatly and inertly on the reel. Stretchy materials, such as nylon, can create a mess, as they contract and expand under tension. Worst of all is monofilament. Do not use spinning line for backing; it can damage the spool of a delicate fly reel as it seeks to expand after being wound under tension. It is all right to use a length of oval monofilament as shooting line behind a shooting head, provided it is not overly long, and is buffered by plenty of dacron or similar backing.

The amount and strength of backing is a function of two things: the capacity of the reel and the task at hand. For typical dry-fly outfits, twenty-pound-test backing is about right. Fifteen-pound test may be used with very light outfits, such as two-weights. For heavier-weight outfits, such as those used for salt water and salmon fly fishing, thirty-pound backing is recommended, and lots of it—two hundred or even three hundred yards. One hundred yards of backing is adequate for the average situation, and even less for the ultralights.

Besides its obvious role in fighting large fish, backing serves to augment the arbor of the reel and help fill the spool. This is quite important. Suppose one were to attach the fly line directly to the arbor, with no backing. Unless the reel were considerably undersized, the line would only partially fill the spool. This results in reduced diameter, which makes reeling in line a tedious chore. Also, the line is wrapped in tight coils, and tends to kink. Ideally, one should attach sufficient backing to fill the spool to the point where the fly line fits comfortably and just about fills the spool, but with enough clearance that the line is not crowded by the frame of the reel when fully wound.

You will notice that most fly reels are quite flat in shape. They are designed that way to make the backing and line spool more or less vertically, rather than laterally, as is the case with bait-casting reels. This helps minimize snarls and tangles, there being no level-wind device to neatly distribute line as it is retrieved. Reels used for heavier work are less critical in this regard, since the lines and backings are of greater diameter and less likely to snarl.

I have learned through experience that a good quality, adjustable drag system is of great importance in fly reels. Even for the small-stream, small-fish angler, the drag system serves a function; it keeps the line from overwinding or backlashing when it is being stripped from the reel. I have found that something more than a simple click device is required. For those who pursue large gamefish, an efficient drag system is a must. I once made the mistake of going after silver salmon in Alaska with a reel that did not have an adjustable drag, and I still bear the scars on my knuckles to remind me of the experience. I also lost several fish to backlashes.

Fly reels require a little maintenance. They should be stripped of line and backing, disassembled, and cleaned with a solvent once a year, or more frequently, if heavily used. Lubrication of the spindle, drag system and other moving parts is also required. For this I recommend teflon grease. Don't overdo it, and thoroughly clean off all excess; you don't want that stuff to get onto your fly line.

At one time a fair amount of attention was given to matching the weight of a fly reel to the rod. The idea was that with the reel mounted, the rod should balance at the front of the cork grip. This is no longer accorded much significance, chiefly because graphite rods are so light that such a balance point is difficult if not impossible to achieve. While using a very heavy reel with a very light rod is not recommended, I wouldn't worry much about balance beyond that.

Before we leave reels, a few thoughts about capacity. I have found that most manufacturers overstate the capacity of their reels by at least one line size. In other words, a reel that is rated for a five-weight line and one hundred yards of twenty-pound-test backing may be overfilled to the point where the line rubs against the frame or perhaps simply won't fit, even when forced.

There are several remedies, the best of which is to select a reel with sufficient capacity, even if it means going up a size. Failing that, you can either reduce the amount of backing, or shorten the fly line. The latter entails cutting off some of the running line at the tail end: ten feet, fifteen, perhaps even twenty. The average line is about ninety feet long, and removing a conservative amount won't hurt anything. Of course, you won't want to do this with a double taper line, as that would destroy one end.

The Support System

One of the ancillary benefits of fishing the dry fly exclusively is that one doesn't have to carry a lot of stuff astream. There are, however, a few items that are essential, or at least very helpful. Let's list them in that manner:

Essential

1. Clippers
2. Stiletto
3. Spare tippet material and assorted monofilament for rebuilding leaders
4. Floatant
5. Hook sharpener
6. Your flies, of course

Very Helpful

1. Hemostats or fine-nosed pliers
2. Drying patch

3. Desiccant
4. Small scissors
5. Strike-indicator yarn
6. A small towel

The clipper can be a plain old pair of nail clippers or one of the specialty tools sold in fly shops. The latter offer the added convenience of a built-in stiletto, without which I suggest a medium-sized safety pin pinned to your shirt or fly vest. Why is the stiletto on the "essential" list? Try threading a fly that has head cement in the eye, a circumstance all too commonly encountered.

Repairing the front end of a leader and replacing tippets comes with the territory in fly fishing. I don't consider it necessary to carry heavy leader material astream, just those diameters required to renew the forward sections.

Wonderful as modern monofilament is, the packaging is lousy, at least at this writing. You may wish to purchase a dispenser that keeps the spools of material neat and organized. A good one is available from Roe Manufacturing Company of Benton, Kentucky. Respooling the material is required, but this is easily done with the help of a variable-speed, 1/4-inch drill. There is also a specially-adapted plastic box available that holds four spools; more convenient, but bulkier, and with less capacity.

An alternative is to purchase some rubber "O" rings at a hardware

The business end of a Roe leader dispenser. The numbers represent the "X" diameter of the material.

store and slip two of them around the material on each spool, with the mono feeding out between them. This was recently suggested by some unheralded genius in one of the fly-fishing magazines. It is one hell of a great innovation.

Some people might not agree that floatant is essential, but I consider it so, as few dry flies will stay on top of the water for very long without it. You have the choice of paste or liquid. Paste is more convenient and doesn't spill or evaporate. Liquid applies itself in a thin, even coat and the solvent does double duty as a cleaner, removing fish slime that will sink the best of flies. If you opt for liquid, get one of the handy bottle-and-harness rigs that clip to the vest. The one in the photo is mine. I slapped together that lash-up for suspending the bottle cap, but now such a device can be purchased at modest cost.

You will definitely want to carry a hook sharpener. With chemical sharpening, today's dry-fly hooks are generally quite sharp as they come from the factory, but they don't stay that way forever. The bony mouths of fish, and incidental contact with rocks, bushes and such, all will take their respective tolls. A small stone or ceramic wafer is okay, but I prefer a diamond sharpener, as it will enable you to touch up your knife and scissors as well.

My method of choice for carrying liquid flotant.

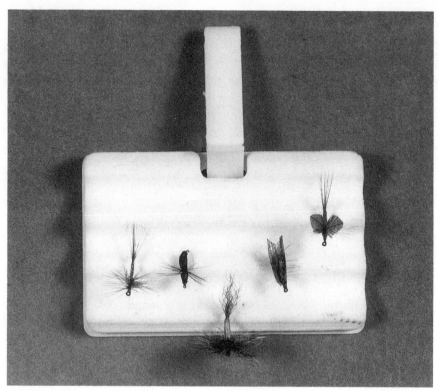

The foam fly patch does a better job than the old lamb's-wool patch, especially with de-barbed hooks.

Now for the "very helpful" list. Hemostats serve several functions, unhooking fish being the main one. Even better than hemostats are needle holders, because the surfaces of the jaws are flat, rather than ridged. They can be used for pinching down the barbs of hooks and holding on to small flies when tying knots. This eliminates the need for fine-nosed pliers. Performing these operations with a ridged-jaw instrument may result in damage to the hook. If you want to carry a ridge-jawed hemostat, take along the pliers, also.

A drying patch is that little piece of absorbent material that pins to the shirt or vest. Traditionally, it was made of lamb's wool. A ripple foam version was recently introduced, which comes as good news to the lambs. The old wool patch was a liability in several respects. The foam patch is better, especially for dry flies. It holds hooks more securely, and in a position where the hackles aren't crushed.

Desiccant is highly absorbent, powdery stuff. It is great for drying and primping a soaked fly and prepares it for reapplying the floatant. I carry mine in a common film canister.

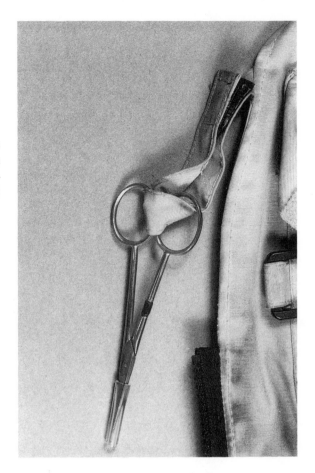

A little loop with Velcroed ends holds scissors nicely. Note the piece of tubing that protects the points— and the angler!

Small scissors have a number of uses. There are times when it is desirable to alter the appearance of a fly with a bit of discreet trimming. A fly can thus be made to appear smaller, daintier and of different character.

Today, I need scissors more for working on strike indicator yarn than for any other purpose. Strike indicators with dry flies? You bet! This will come in for detailed discussion later. If you become an indicator addict, as have I, you will want to carry a paste floatant for treating the yarn.

Why it took me thirty years I can't say, but finally I began to carry a small towel astream. It is attached to the wading vest with a large safety pin. No more fish-slime hands gooing up everything they touch. What a blessing!

In closing, a few words about fly boxes. I recommend compartmented boxes for dry flies, rather than foam ones. Dry flies are not damaged when carried in compartments, provided they aren't crammed in too tightly, so get boxes that accommodate the sizes of flies you want to carry in them, and don't overcrowd. Also, don't purchase boxes with tiny little compartments for carrying miniflies; you won't be able to get your fingers into them. An alternative to the traditional fly vest-fly box arrangement is the self-contained modular fly-box system. It can virtually replace the vest, or at least deload it significantly. The Hatch, depicted here, is a very good one.

The Hatch (registered trade name).

Leaders

THE TWO MAIN FUNCTIONS OF THE LEADER ARE TO FORM AN IN-conspicuous connection between the fly and the end of the fly line, and to pass along the energy developed in the cast, thereby efficiently delivering the fly.

THE ANATOMY OF A LEADER

Leaders are made of monofilament material. Like fly lines, most leaders are tapered. The butt section, which connects to the fly line, is the heaviest; the remainder of the leader tapers progressively to a fine front section, known as the tippet.

The length and strength of the leader varies with the task at hand: the size of the fish one expects to hook, the size of the fly to be cast, and the prevailing water and weather conditions. For example, fishing a faster stretch of water with broken currents, using a large, bushy fly, requires a fairly short leader and stouter tippet; typically, eight feet tapered to 3X. On the other hand, casting a small fly onto a placid stream calls for a longer leader and fine tippet. Ten, twelve, even fourteen feet of leader may be required, and a tippet as fine as 6X or 7X.

The Language of Leaders

The "X" business is a system for rating the diameter of leader material. I'm not sure when or where it originated. Frankly, I believe life would be less complicated if thousandths of an inch were used, but I won't attempt to change the world, at least not in this book. For purposes of clarity, let's match the X ratings with their corresponding diameters in thousandths:

0X	.011
1X	.010
2X	.009
3X	.008
4X	.007
5X	.006
6X	.005
7X	.004

As can be seen, the higher the "X" number, the finer the diameter. There is 8X material available, and with modern monofilament, it is practical. Even so, I would counsel not going lower than 7X, as the 8X is difficult to handle. As a practical matter, I find that 6X will suffice for all but the most critical situations.

I hate to bring this up, but it is so important that I must; be aware that leaders and monofilament materials are not necessarily the diameters marked on the spools. Manufacturers have improved in this respect in recent years, but there are still significant variations. In the butt section, a discrepancy of a thousandth or so isn't critical, but it is when one is down to 6X, or when trying to rebuild the front end of a leader. I use a micrometer to measure mono, and re-mark the spools as necessary. Actually, it's best to take a "mike" with you and measure the mono in the store before buying it. Some shop owners are rather vexed by this, but they shouldn't be.

Choosing the Right Leader

Great advances have been made lately in leader manufacture, and today's over-the-counter leaders are quite satisfactory. They are available in a wide range of lengths and diameters. Selection is based on the angling situation one plans to encounter, and the weight of the fly line. A leader that will match up properly with, let us say, an eight-weight line is a little different from one that will be optimal for a three-weight.

I want the butt diameter of a leader for a five- or six-weight line to be about .020 inches. For seven- and eight-weights, I prefer .022, and for nine-weights, .024. Going in the other direction, I suggest .018 for four-weights, .017 for three-weights and .016 for two-weights. These are rules of thumb, and slight variances are permissible; in fact, the diameters of the front ends of fly lines can vary, even within the same weight class.

Braided Butt Considerations

Today, not all leader butts are made of monofilament; we now have the braided butt. The structure of this material is a woven tube, similar to the Mylar tubing used for some streamer-fly bodies. It acts like a Chinese finger trap, seeking to grip whatever is inside it when outward tension is exerted. Thus, the tip of a fly line can be worked up into the butt, a bit of super glue applied, and a strong connection formed.

There are pros and cons regarding braided-butt leaders. The main ones are:

Pros

1. Butt section always straight; no need to stretch or apply friction.
2. Limpness of material facilitates casting a tighter loop.
3. Stretchiness acts as shock absorber, cushioning strikes.

Cons

1. Limpness a liability in wind, or when casting larger flies.
2. Material very conspicuous on water; exceedingly long tippet required.
3. Braid tends to "wick" up water and drag fly under on pickup.
4. Name-brand braided-butt leaders *very* expensive.

You will have to make up your own mind about the braided butt. Some folks like it. At this writing, I'm not among them.

Knotted or Extruded?

Another choice facing the fly fisher is: extruded knotless leaders or knotted leaders? There was a time not long past when I would have given the extruded leaders pretty bad marks, but they have made enormous strides. Most commercial leaders are of the extruded type, but there are also knotted ones available. The choice is yours. Designs and materials do vary, so shop around and try to get some advice from those with experience.

One thought. If you intend to fish water that contains a large amount of vegetation—Montana's Big Horn River is a prime example—the fewer knots in your leader, the better. Knots tend to collect subaquatic plant life, and this can create serious problems.

A viable compromise is using an extruded leader and adding a tippet. The knot(s) required for this are easy to learn; I'll mention a few of them in a bit. Mastery of these knots, and a cursory familiarity with taper design theory enables the angler to vary at will both the length and tippet diameter of a leader.

Home Made Leaders

Facility with a few simple knots enables you to make your own leaders easily, quickly and inexpensively. In addition to the knot-tying skills, you will need some spools of suitable monofilament in assorted diameters and a set of guidelines for making leaders of various lengths and designs. A number of companies offer kits that include appropriate materials and instructions. Keep in mind that if you are a reasonably active angler, you'll go through the finer diameters that comprise the forward sections of the leader faster than the thicker ones, which are virtually permanent. You will want to carry spools of lighter mono in your wading vest, in order to change tippets and rebuild leaders astream.

An important point is that leader material varies considerably in stiffness, stretchiness and texture. For example, Maxima is considerably stiffer, less stretchy and less slippery than, say Dai Riki, and knots are less likely to slip. The advantage of the Dai Riki-type materials, and this includes Orvis Superstrong, Umpqua and others, is their superior strength-to-diameter ratio. This is a great benefit in dry-fly fishing, where extremely fine tippets are often relied upon to hold sizeable fish. I would, however, counsel against its use in big-quarry fishing, such as salmon on the dry fly, where tippet diameters aren't as critical. The better knotting characteristics and less stretchiness make Maxima or something similar the choice here.

I've found that in smaller diameters, the double surgeon's knot is much more dependable than the blood knot for joining sections—and, it is far superior to the blood knot for tying a Dai Riki-type tippet to a Maxima main leader. Please heed this—it will save you a great deal of frustration.

FURTHER CONSIDERATIONS

Earlier we touched upon some factors for determining what sort of leader will perform best under a particular set of conditions. Let's wade into the subject a little deeper. The following is a list of the most important factors:

1. Size of fly.
2. Clarity of water.
3. Character of water-speed of current and relative calmness or roughness.
4. Wind, or lack of it.
5. Type of day—bright and clear, dark and overcast, whatever.
6. Characteristics of the fish—spooky and wild, freshly-stocked and gullible, and so forth.
7. Behavior of the fish—rising aggressively, rising perfunctorily, not rising but at feeding stations, et cetera.
8. Distance of cast to reach fish.

These factors are so interactive that an absolute prioritization is neither wise nor possible. I will say that presentation is the name of the game in dry-fly fishing, which implies the ability to consistently place a fly on the water with accuracy, and usually, delicacy. If you can't cast, let's say, a sixteen-foot leader effectively, you're better off doing a competent job with a twelve footer, or even less.

It is of further importance that the leader, especially the tippet, properly relate to the size and air resistance of the fly being cast. An unduly fine tippet won't deliver a disproportionately large or bushy fly, but there's more to it than that; there is the matter of the knot.

While some knots work better than others, tying on a large fly with very thin monofilament is ill-advised. Knots tend to "hinge" during casting, and are thus weakened. And double indemnity is incurred if it is the type of knot that encircles the head or "neck" of the fly, such as the popular turle. These knots form behind the eye of the hook, and if the eye is proportionately too large, the knot will be pulled through. Very bad. In addition, strikes to large flies are often violent, and ultra-fine tippets may not withstand such stress.

Here are some guidelines for matching fly size to tippet diameter:

Tippet	Hook Size
1X	2, 4, 6, 8
2X	4, 6, 8, 10
3X	6, 8, 10, 12
4X	8, 10, 12, 14
5X	12, 14, 16, 18
6X	14, 16, 18, 20, 22, 24
7X	20 and smaller

The range of feasibility is due to the variance in hooks. Some are considerably heavier than others, even within dry fly parameters, and sizing scales vary somewhat between manufacturers. Salmon dry-fly hooks, such as the Wilson, are significantly larger in comparison to their corresponding numbers in standard models. You will find that a 1X tippet is not too large for a size 6 or even 8.

KNOT CONSIDERATIONS

Any discussion of leaders naturally brings up the subject of knots. There are many excellent references available, including several pamphlets put out by Cortland with easy-to-follow graphics, so we needn't go into great detail here. I will, however, make just a few recommendations.

1. For joining pieces of heavier monofilament, the blood knot.
2. For joining pieces of finer material, the double surgeons' knot.
3. For attaching a very fine tippet to a leader, especially where the difference in diameter is more than two thousandths of an inch, the double surgeons' knot tied with the finer material doubled over.
4. For flies tied on turned-down-eye or turned-up-eye hooks, a knot that forms around the "neck" of the fly, such as the improved Turle or the double Turle.
5. For flies tied on straight-eye hooks, a knot that forms in front of the eye, such as the improved clinch knot. It is also okay to use such a knot with TDE and TUE hooks, provided the angle of deflection isn't too severe.
6. For attaching a leader butt to a fly line, either the nail knot or needle knot.

4

Fly Designs

WITHIN THE REALM OF THE FLOATING FLY ONE ENCOUNTERS NOT only a vast array of patterns, but also many variations in type, style, and design. This can be confusing.

The term "pattern" refers to the color and texture of a fly, and to a degree, it's composition. There is some overlap between pattern and design. For example, the pattern name "Royal Wulff" brings to mind certain colors and textures (pattern), and also a vision of prominent white hair wings, a deer-hair tail and a generous amount of hackle (design).

Patterns number in the hundreds; in fact, thousands. Designs, at the functional level, number in the teens, or possibly the twenties, if one wishes to stretch the point. Let's focus our discussion there.

The Standard Dry Fly

Anglers who fish various and diverse waters differ as to what they consider a standard dry fly. Here, I refer to the classic type of fly that nheodore Gordon is credited with transplanting from England about a century ago. It is often called the Catskill style, but such a regional definition is far too confining. This type of fly is commonly fished all over the North American continent, and indeed, the world. It is still the most popular of all designs.

The classic dry fly has four components: wings, tail, body and hackle. The tail and hackle shoulder the primary burden of making the fly float; or at least, that's what the angler would prefer. In practise, the body also gets very much involved. In ideal conditions, a well-tied dry fly, dressed with an effective flotant, can be induced to ride high on the hackle and tail for a while, but sooner or later, it will dampen to the point where the hackles will penetrate the surface film, and the fly will ride on its body.

To abet flotation, the hackle and tail are, or should be, fashioned of feathers having the stiffest, strongest barbs. These are always in short supply and compromise is inevitable. Even so, one has a right to expect reasonably good-quality materials in an over-the-counter fly, and that is one of the primary criteria when making selections at the fly shop. Hold the fly up to the light. Do the hackles shine and glisten, at least somewhat? Drop the fly onto a countertop. Is it alive and bouncy? These things are basic, and important.

Look for proper proportions. A classic dry fly should have hackles that are about $1\frac{1}{2}$ times the gap of the hook, wings that extend slightly beyond the perimeter of the hackle, and a tail about as long as the hook itself, or a bit longer. When the fly sits on the counter on the tips of the hackle and tail, the hook point should just about touch the surface, or clear it ever so much. Some variance is allowed here.

Flies designed for heavy currents may have more substantial bodies, whereas those intended for average and slow currents should be more slender. Some of the most successful dressings ever, such as the Quill Gordon, the Red Quill and the Ginger Quill, feature very neat, sculptured bodies made of delicate quills from peacock tail or rooster feathers. This design represents an attempt to closely simulate the shape, shade and markings of certain aquatic insects. Such delicate bodies should have some sort of protective coating. When tying, I coat my quill bodies with super glue. You can do the same with store-bought flies. Inspect them to see if the the bodies are already coated. If they aren't, take a wooden toothpick and apply a thin layer of super glue, such as Zap-A-Gap. If that seems too messy, use fly-tying head cement or, in a pinch, good-quality clear nail polish.

On a classic fly, the two main functions of the wings are to represent the wings of a natural insect, and to act as an airfoil to influence the fly to light on the water in an upright position, properly cocked. For this reason, the wings should be neither too long nor too bulky; either aberration can cause the fly to tip over on its side or face, and make the fly heavier than is necessary. In addition, overdressed wings imbue a fly with an indelicate appearance and distort its intended size. Conversely, underdressed wings contribute neither aerodynamics or silhouette, and simply don't fill their intended role.

Some "standard" dry flies: (1) cut or burned hackle-tip wing, dubbing body, (2) duck or goose quill wing, peacock quill body, (3) wood duck wing, dubbing body, (4) wood duck wing, stripped hackle quill body.

A well-proportioned, well-balanced dry fly at rest.

THE HAIR-WINGED DRY FLY

The only principal difference between a standard and hair-winged fly is the composition of the wings. In fact, some hair-winged flies are adaptations of standard patterns, the Royal Wulff being a prime example. Lee Wulff is credited with originating the hair wing around 1930, the idea having been to fashion a more rugged and conspicuous type of wing that would hold up and be visible in the roily currents of such rivers as New York's Esopus Creek and Ausable River. Today's great number of hair-winged flies, some of which bear Lee's name, are a testimony to his success. They are favorites for fishing fast water and broken currents the world over, and serve double duty as excellent dry flies for Atlantic salmon.

The king of all hair-wing dry flies: the Royal Wulff.

Typically, these flies are more heavily dressed than the classic standard types. They are more generously hackled, have more fibers in the tail, more material in the body and perhaps also in the wings. But the wings can be overdressed. Hair is heavy and bulky, as fly-tying materials go, and too much of it causes problems. It is difficult to say exactly how much is too much. If you notice that a fly constantly tips over, or that the wings overwhelm the appearance of the fly, it is probably overdressed. A little discreet pruning with fine-tipped scissors solves the problem.

COMPARADUN FLIES AND SPARKLE DUNS

Comparaduns are a variation of the hair-wing style. As best as I can determine, they evolved in New York's Adirondacks in the 1930s. Francis Betters, a prominent fly tyer and shop proprietor in the region, ties a fly called the Haystack, which bears close resemblance to the Comparaduns popularized and developed in recent years by angling authors Al Caucci and Bob Nastasi. Francis writes that his father and other local flyfishers used these flies with telling effect.

The Comparadun style features an undivided hair wing. The shaping varies between a "V" and a 180 degree semicircle. In the latter case, the undersides of the wings lie flat on the water while the remainder forms a silhouette suggestive of the wings of the natural. Comparaduns are tied both with and without hackle.

Again, this is a design best suited for rougher currents. That is not to say it will not occasionally work on flat water; practically everything works sometimes. But the silhouette is not sharp, clear and well-defined, making the fly ill-suited for calm waters.

In the mid-1980s, Craig Mathews and his cohorts at Blue Ribbon Flies in West Yellowstone, Montana introduced an innovation. They substituted a polypropylene tail and called the result a Sparkle Dun. The idea is to simulate the image of a mayfly dragging its nymphal shuck while emerging, which many do. These insects are quite vulnerable, and trout are prone to become selective to such easily obtained food. This accounts for the effectiveness of this style of dressing. A similar effect can be gotten by using stiff hackle barbs, which enhance flotation.

Side and front angle views of the Sparkle Dun.

My Hackle Comparadun

A few years ago I began experimenting with Comparaduns tied with hackle wings, rather than hair. The intent was to produce a more delicate fly that could be adapted to small hooks, where hair is too bulky. I also wanted better transmission and reflection of light. These flies have proven to be highly successful. The problem for the non-tyer is that they may be difficult to find in shops; commercial tyers love the hair-winged Comparaduns because they can be tied quickly and with inexpensive materials. A custom tyer could certainly provide them.

DOWN WINGED DRY FLIES

This style of fly is winged with a single bunch of hair, or sometimes other material, that lies over the back of the fly. They have always been popular in the Rockies and the Pacific Northwest as imitations of the stonefly species that abound there. Fly shops in those regions feature an array of patterns such as Bird's Stonefly, the Stimulator, the Sofa Pillow, the Golden Stonefly and the Trude series.

With the fly fishing renaissance of circa 1970, down-winged flies began to proliferate as anglers became aware of the importance of caddis flies, thanks to the writings of Eric Leiser, Larry Solomon, Gary LaFontaine and others. Al Troth, a Pennsylvanian who migrated to Dillon, Montana devised the Elk-Hair Caddis, a murderously effective design.

Two down-wing dry flies: the Hairwing Caddis and the Henryville Special. Both feature "palmered" hackle, which is wrapped over the body.

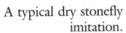

A typical dry stonefly imitation.

The Royal Trude, a down-wing version of the Royal Wulff. This fly is murder on large western rivers.

Concurrently, down-winged fly variations using wing materials other than hair came into prominence. Typical among these are the Henryville Special and the Delta Wing Caddis.

The success of down-winged flies is attributable to their low silhouette, which closely simulates stoneflies and caddis flies. They are also mistaken by the trout for terrestrials, such as grasshoppers and crickets. In addition, they render excellent service as "probing" flies, drawing strikes when fished to likely spots during periods when no hatch activity is in evidence.

Variants

This style of fly is a true high-rider. It employs an oversized hackle: two, three, even four sizes the normal. There are no wings; the upright, prominent hackle fibers comprise a rough wing silhouette. The tails are longer than normal, in order to balance the oversized hackle. The body is small, almost inconspicuous; often a quill of some sort.

In his 1947 classic, *Streamside Guide to Naturals and Their Imitations*, Art Flick popularized the variant style. Three dressings were listed: the Dun Variant, the Cream Variant and the Gray Fox Variant. In his later years, Art fished the Gray Fox Variant almost to the exclusion of everything else. I can understand this; it is a "love" fly, a pattern that can virtually entrance an angler. Variants are dancers; saucy ballerinas performing tiny arabesques and pirouettes on shimmering riffles and glides.

Here again, we have a design best suited to diffused currents. Properly dressed, it is perhaps the most buoyant and high-floating of all, due to the favorable ratio of hackle and tail to hook and body. Like other imprecise flies, it will sometimes produce on slower waters when trout are gorging with abandon on a plentiful hatch, or in failing light.

A variant-style dry fly. Given good-quality hackle, this fly will ride very high on the water, in the attitude shown here.

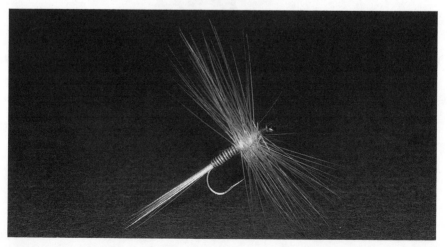

A No-Hackle dry fly, photographed on water. Note the outrigger tails and dramatic wing silhouette.

The No-Hackle Fly

We will now leap from one extreme to the other. The no-hackle, introduced by Doug Swisher and Carl Richards in their landmark 1971 book, *Selective Trout*, is the antithesis of the Wulffs and the Variants. It is a study in minimalism, with its stark, spare, clean silhouette. Quite obviously, its intended arena is the still pool, the quiet flow, where fastidious trout calibrate one's leader tippet and disdain all but the most convincing offerings.

The no-hackle is not an easy fly to properly dress. Certain unconventional techniques are required to obtain balance and floatability, which is limited at best, and few tyers truly possess these skills. The finest no-hackles I have ever seen came from the vises of the Harrop family of St. Anthony's, Idaho. Rene and Bonnie set the standard, and I have recently been informed that their grown children are taking it up. That's wonderful news; such traditions should be carried on.

The construction of the tails, wings and thorax are the keys to the no-hackle. The tails are split wide, acting as outriggers for balance. The wings, which are made of sections from a duck or goose wing feather, are set low and at a wide angle, to enhance balance and contribute to flotation. The thorax is prominent and complements the wings. It is the most important component where flotation is concerned.

There are times, on western spring creeks, eastern limestone streams, British chalk streams and the like, when the no-hackle is a killer. The reason is that the better the visibility and the more time a trout has, the more circumspect a decision the fish will make. An uncluttered image is of the highest importance. These flies do not, however, perform well in rough waters, and I wouldn't try to use them there.

A thorax-style dry fly, with wings shaped by a wing burner, photographed on water.

THE THORAX-STYLE FLY

The thorax-style fly is essentially a modification of the standard dry fly. The tyer cuts away some of the hackle underneath and X-wraps a bit of fur on the underside of the hook directly below the wings as a thorax.

Determining the originator of a style or pattern is often impossible, but there seems to be general agreement that Vincent C. Marinaro, the legendary master of Pennsylvania's intimidating limestone streams, introduced the thorax fly. The unique dressings found in his seminal work, *A Modern Dry-Fly Code* exemplify the thorax concept. *The Code* as it is called, is currently available, having been republished by Lyons & Burford. In my opinion, it is the most original book ever written on the dry fly.

Marinaro's designs are based on visual research done in slant tanks, which enabled him to see from below how flies appeared on the surface, with light coming from above. The image so produced is referred to as a "light pattern." Thorax flies yield a light pattern that is quite similar to that of a natural insect.

On demanding waters, I am very partial to the thorax type of fly. It sits on the surface in a natural-appearing attitude, with the spread hackles acting as outriggers. This results in a highly credible wing silhouette, a very important factor in successful angling on calm water. It floats better than the no-hackle, and the imprints of the hackle barbs on the surface contribute to the attractiveness of the image the fish sees.

The elevated knowledge level of flyfishers today is causing thorax flies to gain in popularity, and some shops do carry a selection. Still, they are not as easily obtained as simpler designs, due to the moderately greater effort and time involved in tying them.

Parachute Flies

This unique design features a hackle that is wrapped horizontally, rather than vertically. Usually, this requires some modification of the wing, so parachutes are not necessarily mere flat-hackled versions of their classic counterparts.

The horizontal hackle produces several interesting phenomena. Because the barbs lie flat, they are more easily supported by water and are less likely to penetrate the surface film, as conventional hackles do. The image from beneath is less cluttered, as less hackle is required for flotation, except in the case of rough currents.

Parachute flies can be tied in different ways to accommodate most types of water. I have enjoyed great success dressing them sparsely and fishing them in quiet stretches. And, they can be pressed into service as spent-fly imitations, thanks to their flat silhouette.

A parachute dry fly, viewed from the top.

Spinners, or Spent Flies

Some of the very best dry-fly fishing is with imitations of imagoes, or fully-adult mayflies. Many species touch the water when depositing their eggs, then drift helplessly on the surface as their ephemeral life ebbs. Usually, this occurs when light is failing and the fish are less mindful of danger. These can be *such* exciting times!

A typical spinner, or spent pattern. Clean, well-defined.

Spinner patterns depend upon several attributes for their effectiveness. Spent flies are extremely translucent, so the tyer must imbue the counterfeits with this quality by choosing materials that readily transmit and reflect light. The wings are typically made of pale hackle barbs or synthetic yarn and the body of sparkly dubbing. Marinaro used seal's hair; today's tyers favor synthetics. The tails should be a la the natural, with only two or three fibers. Spent flies float mainly on their wings and bodies, with little or no contribution from the tails. A skimpy dressing is desired, as most spent fly fishing is done in quiet water, below the riffles and runs where much of the egg laying occurs.

Terrestrials

Many land-based insects end up in the water, for one reason or another. Some, such as the winged ant, simply fly out over the water, for reasons not known to me. Others are blown in by the wind, grasshoppers being a typical example. Still others drop from overhanging branches. These include caterpillars and leaf worms of various types—which all adds up to a trout smorgasbord.

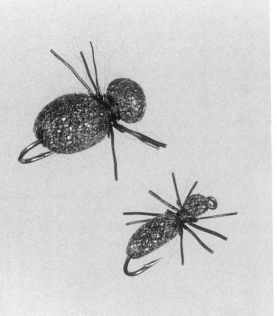 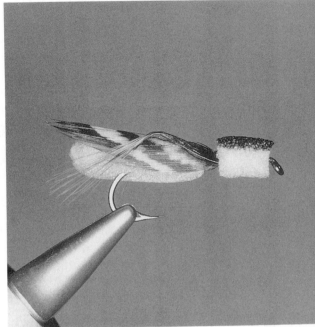

Foam-bodied terrestrials: a beetle, an ant, and a grasshopper.

The two most popular types of terrestrial flies are ant and grasshopper imitations. The latter are generally effective only in hopper country at a time of year when these insects are in evidence. The trout don't have to see many of them to become hopper-conscious. Smaller sizes often, work best.

Ants come in a variety of sizes and colors. As a matter of practicality, most situations can be covered if you carry black ants from size 14 to 20 and brown ones from 16 to 20.

Beetle imitations are productive from spring through fall, in black and brown or copper, from size 12 to 20. If you fish in cricket country, a few medium-sized imitations are deserving of a place in your fly box. Ditto the green leaf worm during warmer months.

In the last few years, closed-cell foam materials have entered the fly fishing and tying market place, and they have virtually revolutionized the tying of terrestrials. These materials float well, come in the right colors and are easily fashioned into ant, beetle, grasshopper and wormlike shapes. I highly recommend foam-bodied terrestrial imitations.

THE HUMPY

Some think of the Humpy as a pattern, with color variations. I prefer to think of it as a unique design. It is far more popular in the Rockies and out West, which I believe is attributable to the old NIH factor: Not Invented Here. It's a terrific fly any time a good floater is required, regardless of region.

The main ingredient in a Humpy is hair: deer, elk or whatever. A generous amount of hackle is also applied. The underbody is made of floss, yarn or similar material, in various colors. The blond Humpy is sometimes called a Goofus Bug.

This is essentially a broken-current fly, but I have had it work on calmer pools when something was hatching that the Humpy matched reasonably well. My preferred colors are greens, olives and yellows, with hackle and hair varied to complement the shade of the underbody. Sizes 12 to 18 are most common.

Recently, I saw some Humpys with foam overbodies, or humps. This is the same stuff most tyers are now using for terrestrials, and I'm sure it works wonderfully well on Humpys. It has the desired floating qualities, is easy to use and is much more durable than hair. This should eliminate the common lament that Humpys are hard to tie.

The preceding covers the most common dry-fly designs at this writing. There are other types of flies around, and of course we can expect continued evolution, what with new synthetics coming along at a rapid pace, and the insatiable curiosity and creativity of the fly-tying contingent. If recent history is any indication, much of this new-fangled stuff will be of questionable, or at best, limited value, but there will also be some that will constitute significant advancements. Open-minded skepticism is a good policy.

Born in the Rockies, the Humpy is a very effective dry fly any place a good floater with a buggy look is called for.

A typical floating nymph. The little ball of closed-cell foam provides a base for the hackle and abets flotation.

Floating Nymphs and Such

In my opinion, a fly doesn't have to look like a Light Cahill or a Royal Wulff to qualify as being a dry fly; all it has to do is float and be fished on the surface. Based on this rationale, I herewith include the floating nymphs and surface emergers that have become so popular in recent years.

Some aquatic insects seem to pop up out of the water and fly away with virtually no hesitation. Others encounter all sorts of problems getting out of their nymphal shucks and becoming airborne. Some of them never make it off the surface. Years ago, Swisher and Richards named them "stillborn duns." This adds up to easy pickings for the opportunistic trout, and potential excitement for the observant angler.

There are many innovations for dealing with this phenomenon. I'll cover just a couple. The floating nymph is self-descriptive. It is a fly that looks like a nymph, but floats like a dry fly. It is usually tied on a light-wire hook and employs materials that contribute to flotation. A common artifice is to attach a little ball of closed-cell foam as an emerging wing, which serves to suspend the fly in the surface film.

The floating emerger might be described as a cross between a nymph and a dry fly. It takes many forms. A typical pattern might feature a translucent tail made out of poly yarn that suggests a dragging shuck and dry fly hackle for floatation. As mentioned earlier, the Sparkle Dun is a form of floating emerger.

The Case for De-Barbing

Possibly you've heard this sermon before, but in case you haven't, or failed to become a believer, here it is again.

My friends, I urge you to fish barbless. I assure you that you will not lose fish; in fact, you'll land a greater percentage of your hookups. Barbs were invented to keep bait from slipping off the hook. As fly fishers, we don't have that problem.

Here are several excellent reasons for going barbless:

1. Better penetration with less force means fewer breakoffs.
2. Much less of a hole in the fish's mouth.
3. Easy, quick unhooking minimizes stress on fish and damage to fly.

Consider that last point, for it is often overlooked. Each year, countless thousands of flies are ruined while being yanked out of the bony jaws of trout. Dry flies aren't cheap these days, and as any tyer will tell you, neither are good materials. So even if you don't believe the part about landing more fish and all that, just think of all those nice flies you'll save. In other words, I don't care why you do it, just do it.

Dry-fly hooks are delicate and must be de-barbed carefully. With a fine-nosed plier or surgical tool, gently pinch down on the barb until it either pops off or is flattened. Don't attempt to flatten the bump where the barb was, as you'll almost certainly damage the hook. Once the barb is gone, you've done enough.

You will undoubtedly hear people say that a high percentage of re-leased trout die. Baloney! Trout that are brought to net with dispatch and handled with care almost always survive the experience in good condition. People who argue against this are either looking for an excuse not to release trout, and/or are badly misinformed. These people are enemies of trout. Be the trout's friend, and you'll be richly rewarded.

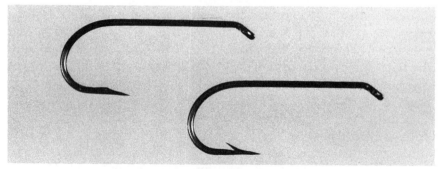

A de-barbed hook and one in its original condition.

Bugs

ONE OCCASIONALLY EXPERIENCES GOOD DRY-FLY FISHING WHEN there are no rising trout and nothing on the water for them to rise to, but usually things go much better when there is food on the surface that can be imitated. Therefore, a basic familiarity with the types of insects one might encounter in trout country is of considerable value.

The following is a mere glimpse of this vast field of study. There are plenty of books available for further research, if one has such inclination, but it isn't necessary to pursue the subject in depth to do well astream and have a good time.

Here, we will simply look at the insects themselves. Techniques for fishing imitations of them will be integrated into the on-the-water chapters to follow.

AQUATIC INSECTS

Aquatic insects live in the water during their immature stages. In this state, they are called nymphs, larvae, or in some cases, pupae. At an appointed time they are transformed into winged insects. This phenomenon is known to anglers as a hatch, or emergence. It is a most important and exciting event.

The three main orders of aquatic insects are the mayflies (Ephemeroptera), the caddisflies (Trichoptera) and the stoneflies (Plecoptera). Others can be important at times, such as damselflies and dragonflies (Odonata), water bugs and beetles (orders Hemiptera and Coleoptera) and the large order of Diptera, which includes those hated pests, the mosquito and the blackfly. But while swatting and cursing, keep in mind that these persistent devils are an important part of the food chain.

SEASONAL CYCLES

With some exceptions (certain stoneflies hatch every two or three years, some Diptera produce several generations per season), aquatic insects hatch once a year, at rather specific times. This predictability enables the informed fly fisher to be prepared for what might be encountered, and to schedule fishing excursions for (hopefully) prime times. But it isn't quite like clockwork; weather and water conditions can accelerate or delay an emergence, both in terms of date and time of day. It is, therefore, wise to allow some flexibility in one's schedule.

MAYFLIES

The mayfly is not necessarily the most prevalent aquatic insect encountered in trout waters, but it certainly is the most familiar. The more common species have nicknames, such as Hendrickson, Pale Morning Dun, Blue-Winged Olive, Green Drake, and fly patterns are named after them. Classic dry fly design is essentially mayfly-oriented.

Mayflies are easily recognizable. They have upright wings, six legs, two or three tails and a cylindrical body. In most cases, a small pair of vestigial wings are found at the base of the main wings. The absence of these is an aid in insect identification, should you decide to get into the entomology of angling.

Mayflies range in size from a few millimeters to nearly thirty millimeters in overall body length. The tiny ones are not to be ignored. They can be just as important as the larger, more succulent ones, and even more so in some cases, as we shall learn.

DUNS AND SPINNERS

Mayflies are unique in that they have two winged states: the *dun* (subadult, subimago) and the *spinner* (adult, imago). They can be of enormous importance in either or both stages, although this varies greatly from species to species.

The dun is the emergent form that pops out of the nymphal shuck and seeks to fly off into the bushes or trees. Those that survive soon shed

A typical mayfly.

A mayfly riding its nymphal shuck after emerging.

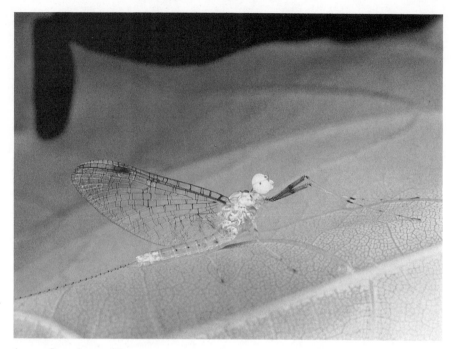

A mayfly spinner. Note transparent wings.

their skins one last time and become spinners. Some get off the water very quickly, others drift and struggle for some time. The latter are beloved by the dry-fly fisher.

The spinner is the sexually mature form that has only one remaining mission: to fertilize the eggs and deposit them in the stream. Spinners are characterized by clear, shimmering wings, elongated tails and enhanced coloration. The transformation is so profound in some mayflies that it is hard to believe the duns and spinners are of the same species. It wasn't many generations ago that only the most informed anglers knew that the so-called Green Drake and Coffin Fly were the dun and spinner of the great eastern mayfly, Ephemera guttulata.

Mayflies truly are ephemeral. Transformation into the final form takes place very quickly, in less than an hour with a few species and usually within no more than a day. Mating and oviposit usually follow shortly thereafter.

You are liable to find mayflies in any type of water, including lakes and ponds. Some occur only in faster water, as movement of the current is required to facilitate breathing and procurement of food. Others live in slow, silty pools.

Spinners instinctively seek to deposit their eggs in the type of current to which that species is indigenous. Quite often, this is fast-moving, riffly water. Some, however, do return to the slower pools to oviposit.

A typical caddis fly.

CADDISFLIES

Caddisflies are the opposite of mayflies in that they go through two subaquatic stages and only one winged stage. First they are worms, usually encased in a protective "house" formed out of bits of detritus, sand and other materials from the streambed. Later, still within the case, they pupate, much as a butterfly forms a chrysalis.

Caddisflies look quite a bit like moths. The wings are tented over the body and are disproportionately longer than the abdomen, as compared to mayflys. Having no subsequent adult stage, they retain this appearance as long as they live, which may be considerably longer than mayflies. Some caddis live for weeks. They also occur in a wide range of sizes, nearly as great as that of the mayfly, and any size can be important at a given time.

While caddis differ in color between species, they are not as individually distinctive as mayflies, and few have colloquial names. An exception is the so-called Shad Fly, a common northeastern caddis that appears just about the time the shad are making their spring spawning run.

While some caddis—particularly those native to the Rockies—ride the water for a ways prior to lift-off, many emerge like submarine-based rockets. Others tend to be hyperactive on the water, jumping about as though the surface were a hot griddle. This calls for different methods on the part of the fly fisher, to be discussed further along.

As with mayflies, caddisflies inhabit a complete range of water types. Most caddis prefer moving currents, but there are slow-pool dwellers and even a few still-water species.

STONEFLIES

Members of the order Plecoptera can be exquisitely beautiful, with mosaic-like markings in sharply contrasting shades. Of the three orders covered so far, they are considerably the least prolific and of the least significance to the dry-fly contingent. However, there are a few species that do cause legendary surface feeding, such as the huge western stone-fly known as the salmon fly because of the orangy pink coloration of its underside.

The giant stoneflies are among the largest aquatic insects, some obtaining a size comparable to a person's little finger. There are also very small stoneflies, such as the tiny dark Capnia that emerge during the winter months.

Stoneflies have two sets of functional wings and are strong, if clumsy, fliers. When the insect is at rest, the wings lie flat along the back, in virtual layers. The bodies are proportionately longer than either of the two orders previously discussed, and are fairly substantial. The head structure is quite massive; nymphs of the larger species have mandibles of sufficient strength to kill other insects and even small fish. The legs of both the nymphs and adults are highly functional, enabling these insects to scamper quickly from danger.

Stoneflies have only two forms, the nymph and the adult. The larger species, which may live as a nymph for three and even four years, shed their shucks numerous times throughout nymph-hood, to accommodate growth.

Stoneflies require a great deal of oxygenation from their habitat and are only found in moving waters. There are a few lacustrine species that inhabit cold northern lakes where wave action, and the insect's ability to do "push-ups," are sufficient to sustain breathing. Some prefer the swiftest of currents, to which they are well adapted by virtue of their powerful legs.

Emerging stoneflies are rarely found on the surface. Their normal hatching procedure is to crawl across the streambed to shore, then out onto a rock or tree, where they may cast their final shuck unseen by the watchful eyes of hungry birds. Many are nocturnal, knowing instinctively that their deliberate style of flight makes them highly vulnerable.

A typical stonefly.

What dry fly fishing there is to stoneflies is brought on by females returning to the river to oviposit. It's a shame there isn't more of this, because when and where it does exist, fishing can be really wild.

MIDGES

In casual angler's vernacular, all small flies get lumped as midges, an inaccurate terminology. True midges are of the order Diptera. It is a huge order and by no means are all of its members small. There are giant craneflies that can practically straddle a tea saucer! But most midges are quite diminutive and occur in prolific numbers. While usually of more interest to the subsurface angler, midges can at times produce excellent, and very demanding, dry-fly fishing. One thing to remember about tiny insects; a trout has to eat a lot of them to make a living. But then, trout often prefer to eat in small bites.

Midges come in various sizes and conformities. Most of the ones commonly encountered while fishing resemble mosquitoes, to which they are closely related. Some have short legs, others have long, gangly

The cranefly, a large midge, or diptera.

ones. They are widely distributed, but tend to prefer slower currents. Some species are highly tolerant of cold and are an important winter food source. Western spring creek flyfishers enjoy some terrific winter fishing to midges when weather conditions allow the more hardy to venture forth.

Sometimes it is difficult to tell that trout are surface feeding on midges. If the insects are present in the air, look for very gentle, almost imperceptible rises in quiet backwaters and side currents. Usually, this is a morning occurrence.

DAMSELFLIES

There are several species of damselflies commonly encountered in trout waters. These gorgeous Zygopterae usually come in luminous greens and blues, and prefer the still waters of lakes and ponds. Look for them around lily pads. Large, quiet pools in rivers may also have significant populations.

As an Easterner, I was always aware of damselflies in bass and panfish ponds, but never thought of them as significant trout food, because there

A type of damselfly.

were no trout ponds where I grew up. Eventually, my travels took me to the Rockies, and there I fell in love with the dry damselfly. True, it's a better bug for nymphers, but wonderful surface action can be had when conditions are proper.

I still have not experienced dry-fly fishing to the damselfly's close relative, the dragonfly. But who knows? It may be happening some place.

TERRESTRIALS

As was mentioned in the chapter on artificial flies, certain types of land-based insects do find their way into the water, sometimes in great numbers, and stimulate superb dry-fly fishing. The two most often encountered are ants and grasshoppers.

Grasshoppers come in quite a range of sizes and colors, so pay attention to those you see near the water. Prime hopper fishing occurs on windy days, when naturals are blown into the rivers. Many streams don't offer much in the way of hopper fishing, because there are few or no naturals in the area, or water conditions are poor during grasshopper season.

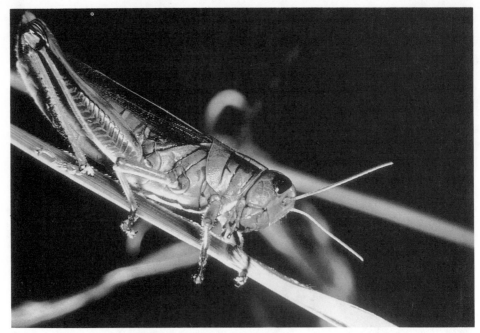

A typical grasshopper.

It is important, particularly if you are a traveling angler, to realize that grasshopper populations tend to be rather cyclic. A bonanza of hoppers in, let's say, August of a given year doesn't mean there will be a similar occurrence the following year. I wouldn't advise planning an expensive trip around hopper fishing, great as it can be. It's one of those things to be taken advantage of when it happens, and to be thankful for.

Ants may be found at various times throughout the season and trout seem to be constantly aware of them. I have had some amazing and exciting times with ant imitations. Sometimes I will fish them to rises when I can't get the trout to take what I see on the water, or can't determine what they are rising for. Usually this works, don't ask me why.

Ants come in a variety of sizes and colors. As mentioned in the chapter on artificial flies, most situations can be covered if you carry black ants from size 14 to 20 and brown ones from 16 to 20.

Ants that are involved in reproduction are called sexuals and grow wings at mating time. This phenomenon can precipitate fantastic dry-fly fishing, as the swarms often fly out over water, for some reason. Trout find them so desirable that I have actually seen them switch from feeding on a hatch to gulping the winged ants greedily. This has happened to me several times when float-tubing a trout lake or pond. It's a good idea to carry some winged ants; these flights are difficult to anticipate, and usually not of long duration.

Beetles are also a favorite of trout and imitations will often produce from spring through fall. Black beetles from size 12 to 20 are of great value. If you fish in areas where Japanese beetles occur, some coppery ones may come in very handy. These insects are not so plentiful as they were in the years immediately preceding and following World War II due to the effective controls that were developed, but there are still some around, and now and then they make for great fishing.

Other terrestrials of note include crickets and various leaf worms and tree hoppers. There used to be a great many green leaf worms in the Northeast during warmer months. I don't see nearly as many of these as I did years ago; perhaps pollution has taken its toll. I recall some wonderful action on my home Catskill streams, and it still happens on occasion.

Japanese beetles at a picnic.

PART TWO

ON THE WATER

NOW IT'S TIME TO TAKE TO THE STREAM—OR RIVER, LAKE, pond, whatever. You may prefer, or be limited to, a certain type of water, but the fact is that dry flies work on practically all types of water. When circumstances are conducive, the floating bug can be fished on dead-calm ponds, rushing currents one can't stand up in, and everything in between.

The first section of the book dealt with orientation; this will deal with the trout's world. We'll learn to understand the fish's realm, and the fish themselves. We will examine how they surface-feed, and why they do it the way they do. We will explore the many variations that are encountered in this type of fishing—practically infinite, but with very important commonalities and interactions.

Essentially, the water will dictate how you approach the quarry and present your fly. In legitimate golf, one plays the ball as it lies, and the course dictates how each shot is played. This proposition is even more true in fly fishing. We must "play" the fish as *it* lies, and there are no allowances for ground under repair, television cables or winter rules. The trout does not allow itself to be dropped a rod's length away, where it's easier to pitch a fly at him.

Of course, the general picture also plays an important role; the presence of insects, types of rise forms, light, shade and so forth. We shall look at all of this. But since our efforts—in fact, our entire set of strategies—are so disciplined by the water, I have chosen to structure this portion of the book around that element. We shall enter these diverse currents and learn how to cope with the situations they present.

About Trout

IT IS OF GREAT VALUE TO THE DRY-FLY FISHER TO UNDERSTAND trout. Their situation is terribly simple: to eat, and not be eaten. Therefore, a trout needs a relatively safe lie where there is protection from predators and access to food. The better the lie, the more likely it is to be occupied by a trout of interesting size.

The fly fisher—particularly the dry fly fisher—needs to realize that trout are awfully apprehensive of what goes on above, and understandably so; flying creatures have been chewing them up for eons. Any movement from above may be perceived as clear and imminent danger. This means we must be most discrete in how we move about.

Trout are less afraid of things in the water than of threats from overhead. After all, it's their environment, and they know they can quickly swim to safety. This is not to say that wading doesn't scare fish; it definitely does. But many times I find that, with due care, I can wade to within easy casting range of trout. In some cases, they will tolerate amazing proximity. Yet I often see these same fish spook at a line being cast in the air above them.

Today, situations exist that lull the angler into a false sense of security, and result in lack of due caution. In many areas, all or most of the trout are hatchery products, rather than stream-born natives. When freshly stocked, they may actually react in a positive manner to the presence of humans, as they associate us with food. Stocked trout that survive gradually acclimate and develop their dormant protective instincts, but even so, they can remain highly tolerant, particularly those that see lots of anglers.

Under certain circumstances, even stream-born trout that have never been fed by the hand of man can become acclimated to our presence. The famous western spring creeks get fished steadily, if not heavily, throughout the course of the season. These trout see people in close proximity from the time they leave the egg, and become quite indifferent to all but the most disruptive encroachment.

There's the old saying, "familiarity breeds contempt." It also breeds carelessness and bad habits in fly fishers. We spend a lot of time fishing for hatchery-reared trout or people-conditioned trout. Then we find ourselves in a more natural situation, and we don't know how to behave. My advice is, treat all trout as though they are naturally wild and spooky. You'll do better in any situation.

Keep in mind that a trout can be somewhat scared and intimidated without necessarily streaking for cover. There are reasons for this behavior. Most, if not all animals have a buffer zone, a perimeter of tolerance. They may be aware of a potentially threatening presence outside of this zone, but do not react, because they instinctively know they can escape. Think about a robin hunting worms on your lawn. Fifty feet away, you are trimming the hedges. The bird knows you are there, yet goes on with it's business. You move ten feet closer, and it flies.

Trout will behave in the same manner. A hatch is on, and fish are surface-feeding. You are standing knee-deep, thirty feet away, casting. In all probability, the trout are very much aware of your presence, but don't interpret it as clear and imminent danger. You wade a little closer, trying for a better vantage point. The fish go down.

I further believe, based on my experience and observation, that while trout will continue to rise with anglers close at hand, they do so with heightened caution and discretion. I think this accounts for much of the frustration we encounter when we repeatedly pass a perfectly believable fly over feeding fish, getting excellent floats, and are refused, even ignored. The trout, with its miniscule brain, can't actually conceive of fly fishing, but it can make associations and, I believe, can correlate the slightly different-looking bug that keeps drifting by with that strange tree-like form in the stream a short distance away.

Do trout learn from the experience of being caught and released? Absolutely! But sometimes they do dumb things anyway. One afternoon, while fishing a heavy Hendrickson hatch on the Beaverkill, I hooked and was broken off by a good-sized trout. Ten minutes later, my friend Russell waded into the area, made two casts and hooked and landed that very trout, an eighteen-inch wild brown, with my Red Quill firmly embedded in its jaw. The feeding urge overwhelmed the alarm and discomfort of being hooked and played.

It is also useful to know that despite their similarities in appearance and penchant for group behavior, trout can differ remarkably as individuals. Some are simply much smarter, within the limits of trout intelligence.

Another war story. When the Henry's Fork of the Snake River in eastern Idaho was in its heyday, it held an amazing number of large rainbow trout. As rainbows go, they were quite cerebral, and usually the angler had to do everything right to catch them. One day I was fishing the Pale Morning Dun hatch with what looked to me to be a close imitation. I was encountering high selectivity and exhaustive scrutiny, and was delighted to be able to hook the occasional trout, as few of the anglers around me were fooling any at all.

A large trout began to feed in a channel about twenty feet in front of me; close, but with some mean cross-currents in between. I got a "junk" cast to fall nicely, resulting in about a one-foot float. The fish took, jumped, and immediately dove into the weeds. I got directly downstream and kept gentle yet steady pressure on the 6X. After a while, the trout backed itself out, and the battle turned in my favor. She went about twenty inches, a heavy-bodied female.

I removed five flies from her mouth, one of which was my PMD. The other four were all different and, for that particular hatch, all wrong. A couple of them were large attractor flies, usually worse than useless on this water. All appeared to be fresh. I believe the only reason I was able to move this fish out of the weeds was that she was tired from recent exertions; yet she was still feeding with abandon.

This was a dumb fish. She had attained great size through a fortuitous combination of good luck, an inexhaustible food supply and the largesse of catch-and-release anglers.

Depending on geography, you'll be fishing for brown trout, rainbow trout, brook trout and cutthroats of several strains. Browns are noted for their superior intelligence and wariness. Rainbows are generally less cautious and reticent. Brook trout have a reputation for being compulsive and easily fooled. Cutthroats, particularly the Yellowstone strain, are often perceived as being the most gullible of all.

But let me tell you something; I've cast to nine-inch brookies in the Battenkill that turned up their snouts at my best presentations and made me want to cry. And I've seen those cutthroats at Buffalo Ford in Yellowstone Park, so accommodating on opening day, become next to uncatchable only a few weeks later. It is not wise to generalize. Things change.

Enjoy those naive trout; they will make you look good and feel good. But approach all trout as though they are the epitome of erudition, and your results will be greatly improved.

SURFACE FEEDING

As a dry-fly addict, you will be analyzing and trying to interpret rise forms and surface-feeding behavior for the rest of your angling career. Rises are always an indication that fish are feeding at or near the top, but exactly what they're taking and how they're taking is another matter. Here are a few thoughts to start you on your journey.

First, understand that trout don't work any harder than they have to. Unlike humans, they do not indulge in exertion just for the fun of it. The concept of running a marathon as weekend recreation would never occur to a trout. They position themselves to feed with the least amount of effort, and as a rule, *they generally take their food in its easiest and most readily available form.*

Like many predators, trout often go for cripples; they're simply easier to catch. A large trout will ignore a group of small bait fish nearby, but if one of them starts to behave as though it is injured, in a flash, the trout will turn on it. All good streamer-fly fishers are aware of this.

It's often the same with insects. Trout just love to feed on emergers, shuck-draggers, and spent flies that have fallen onto the water for the last time. If there are classic-looking duns present, this behavior can be misleading. The angler sees the rise forms and the drifting duns, but fails to realize that the trout are selective to the emerger. Instead of changing to a fly with a different image, the angler ties on various patterns, fools with the leader tippet and swears a lot.

One indication of whether or not trout are taking insects on the surface is the presence or absence of a bubble in the rise form. Usually, a little air is sucked in when a fish takes on the surface and is expelled through the gills in the form of a bubble. Foolproof? No, but highly indicative.

Once you have established that trout are indeed taking insects on top, the next step is to determine the form. Sometimes this is simple—one matches the hatch, the trout take the proffered fly, and all is bliss. But often what appears to be a straightforward situation can be most deceptive. We watch a dun go floating by. A trout rises and takes it. We actually see the insect disappear into the fish's mouth! The phenomenon veritably screams "dry fly." We match the insect and proceed to get refused on cast after cast.

Like as not, such trout are feeding on shuck-draggers; flies that are having trouble emerging. If you carry a little net astream, capture a few bugs when this type of feeding is going on and you will see the nymphal shuck hanging off the rear. This can be imitated with a particular type of fly, such as the Sparkle Dun described in the chapter on fly design.

Sometimes insects are hyperactive on the water when trying to become airborne. I've observed mayflies struggling, and caddisflies hopping about as though they were on a hot plate. Often, this induces violent rise forms.

The dry-fly angler is well-advised to simulate insect behavior. Sometimes a very subtle twitch is enough to make the difference. When caddis are doing their dance, an effective ploy is to cast directly on top of a rise form. Immediately and with some emphasis "pop" the fly onto the water. The trout takes it for the bug that just escaped, and attacks.

Spinners and Spents

The presence of spent flies on the water can present the dry-fly fisher with golden opportunities. Again, it's the kill-the-cripple thing. The trout know these flies aren't going anywhere. Some insects oviposit in slower waters—the eastern green drake is a prime example—but many prefer to drop their eggs in the runs and riffles, where requisite oxygenation is present. The insects then fall spent onto the water and are swept into the pool below, where the trout await their arrival with alacrity.

So when you observe sipping rise forms, particularly in the latter part of the day, think spent. There may be a hatch going on which draws our attention, but is being ignored by the trout in favor of the helpless spents. I've seen this hundreds of times. Try to position yourself near the head of the pool. That is where the better trout will usually be, in prime feeding positions.

Big Fly, Little Fly

In the chapter on insects it was stated that tiny flies could be as important as large flies, or even more so. Let's explore this.

Okay, the availability of large insects on the surface can stimulate surface feeding by huge trout that seldom come to the top, and it can be very exciting. But the average trout may have problems here. An enormous bug, such as a western "salmon fly" or a Michigan Hexagenia, is quite a gulp and may be tough to swallow. Run-of-the-stream trout can get filled up on megabugs in a hurry, especially late in the day, after they've been feeding on other things. And when they are fairly sated, trout tend to eat in small bites, just like people near the end of a substantial meal.

The message is, don't assume that when large insects are on the water, that's always what the trout want. If your megafly imitation is consistently refused, be suspicious and start looking the situation over. Many times I have found that trout were taking some little mayfly or minicaddis while a much larger bug was available.

There are times when small insects are all there are, and for the fish, it's that or nothing. Believe me, they will never opt for nothing. Anglers may dislike tiny flies, but trout don't. Small flies usually hatch in great numbers, and fish must eat lots of them to get enough food. I have watched trout midging on western streams when the insects were so thick the fish took them in bunches, as a whale takes krill. In the peak years on the Henry's Fork, I saw small spents on the water in such numbers that they actually touched each other, and the bank-feeders took them several at a time.

So if you have an antipathy towards small flies, overcome it. With today's leader materials, anyone can successfully fish tiny flies, and deal with the heavy trout that take them.

The preceding dissertation provides some insights into the surface-feeding behavior of trout. Often, it is influenced as much by the water and currents as by the presence of insect life. This we shall examine in the chapters that lie ahead.

PREPAREDNESS

One more piece of orientation. The dry-fly fisher is well-advised to go astream prepared for what might be expected *in that water at that time*. This means being aware of what insects are due to emerge and what water conditions will be encountered.

Few things in this world are more frustrating than standing in a river with trout rising all over the place and not having the right fly. It is also frustrating to try to fish a stretch of water with flies and tackle that aren't well suited to the situation: long, fine leaders and small flies in heavy currents, the opposite in quiet pools. So do your homework, find out about current insect activity and what type of water you'll be fishing, and prepare accordingly.

And now, to the river.

7

The Classic Pool

Let's begin our exploration of dry-fly fishing in what might be considered an archetypical pool. I realize this may mean many things to many people, so let's be more definitive.

This "classic" pool has an easily identified beginning, middle and end, each with its own character. It is a large pool and part of a sizeable trout river. Portions of it are too deep to wade, even in low water.

The two shorelines differ remarkably; one is flat, almost beachlike. The water is shallow at the edge and deepens very gradually. The other shore is bordered by a steep hillside—actually a small mountain—and drops off immediately to unwadeable depth. Thus, a cross section of the pool is quite asymmetrical. Large boulders support the steep bank.

THE RUN AT THE HEAD

Above the pool proper there are about seventy-five yards of fairly fast water. It is wadeable on each side, and crossable in times of moderate water levels. Width averages about fifty yards. The streambed has considerable structure, consisting of stones and rocks from softball to basketball size, with a larger boulder here and there, several of which protrude above the surface during normal flows. Near the head of the run are two bridge abutments; plenty of holding spots for trout, and lots of drift problems for the dry-fly fisher.

Typical structure: the run at the head of the pool.

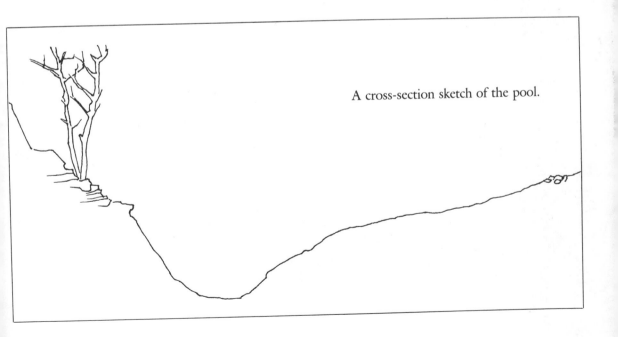

A cross-section sketch of the pool.

← The "classic" pool.

Unless there are steadily rising trout in the main pool, this may be an ideal place to begin your day astream. Slow, flat water doesn't lend itself to prospecting—that is, blind casting—very well at all. Moving water affords the angler a far better opportunity. Because of the gradient, the current is rather fast here, especially in the center. When the water is high, the current is too fast for practical fishing, except possibly around the edges. During normal flows, the pace of the water is such that trout can surface-feed without undue effort.

This stretch is largely, and unwisely, ignored by the average fly fisher in favor of the leisurely pool below, which gets pounded. This is because:

1. The faster, more broken currents make it harder to get a nice float.
2. The trout aren't free risers, like those in the flat water below, so they aren't constantly calling attention to themselves.
3. The structure of the stream is mostly subsurface, making it more difficult to "read" the water.

Because of its diverseness, this type of water affords us an opportunity to become familiar with some of the common terminology of fly fishing. Let's attach a definition to that term: reading water. It means analyzing a

Note the very visible seams on either side of the main tongue of current.

section of stream in terms of its structure, determining where trout lie and what must be done in order to present a fly to them. When there are insects, and trout are rising, that part of the "read" is done for the angler. The fish have shown themselves, and all that remains is to engineer the presentation. But often we are "fishing the water," with no rises in evidence.

We must also understand the meaning of the term "structure," and its importance. In this context, structure refers to the physical composition of a section of stream: the deflections that provide shelter for trout, and respite from relentless currents. Structure is essential; the faster the water, the more so. Trout may move into rapid currents for brief periods to feed on a heavy hatch, but they can't stay there for long without returning to a resting spot, where deflection is present.

Structure can be obvious (a large rock, a bridge abutment), subtle (a small rock or a little pocket in the streambed) and everything in between. Sometimes structure is virtually impossible to identify, as it is hidden by the water itself. It doesn't take much to create a holding spot. I've seen many a good-sized trout comfortably nestled behind a stone the size of a grapefruit.

An overhead-view sketch of the piece of water in the photo showing the various seams and some of the positions from which presentations can be made.

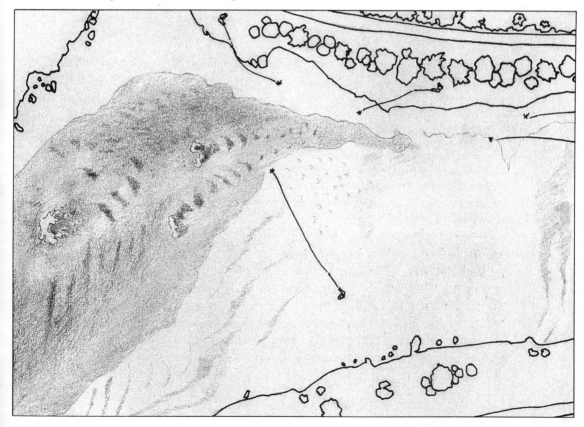

More seams. These are formed by the current interacting with the bank structure.

THE APPROACH

Getting into a run of broken water, such as the one I've just described, doesn't require quite as much stealth as does entering a still pool. The water that obscures the trout also makes it harder for them to perceive us, in two ways: visibly and audibly. The movement diffuses images from outside, and the rushing currents muffle the noises caused by wading.

Even so, stealth is advised. Stay as low as you can. Don't climb up on boulders to get a better view or increase your casting range; the higher the object, the more visible it is through water. Move deliberately and try to wade with the least possible commotion. Crunching gravel and rocks being clunked together telegraph your presence.

There is also the matter of the color of clothing and the flash or reflections given off by certain items of tackle. For the moment, I will simply comment that dull, natural colors are much less conspicuous. The matter of reel and line flash, et cetera, will be addressed when we move to a flat pool, where it becomes far more critical.

Exactly where to enter the water depends on the idiosyncrasies of the particular stretch. If the currents are fairly even, with all or most of the structure subsurface, it might be feasible to fish such a run cross stream. More often than not, however, it is best to approach from below and cast upstream, sometimes directly, sometimes at an angle. Let's assume this is the case in our model.

We are assuming a no-hatch situation here, and are simply going to probe and prospect, fishing the water, casting to spots that should hold trout. However, that is not an assumption that should be made in actual fishing. The first order of business, when approaching any piece of water, is to look for:

1. Feeding fish, and
2. What they're eating.

Sometimes, surface feeding is obvious, with trout busting all over the place. At other times, rises can be incredibly subtle and most difficult to see in broken water. So take time to look the situation over before jumping in.

CHOICE OF FLY

With no emerging insects to guide the angler, choice of fly becomes a discretionary matter. Remember the fly-design chapter, where we discussed the properties of various types of flies. Here, we will want a good floater that has high visibility, both for us and the fish. There are lots of patterns that qualify. Several time-proven classics that seem to work practically everywhere are the Adams, the Light Cahill, the Gray Fox Variant and the Wulff series; the Royal Wulff, the Grizzly Wulff and the Ausable Wulff are all favorites of mine. Or you might opt for a general caddis type, such as the Henryville Special or Troth's Elk-Hair Caddis.

In this type of water, one wouldn't want too small a fly. We want the trout to notice it, and consider it worth the effort required to rise and seize it. But usually, we don't want to go to the other extreme, either. When in doubt, a size fourteen is a pretty safe choice, or perhaps a sixteen, if the water is low and clear. If it appears that a larger image and higher silhouette are called for, the Variant is an excellent selection.

Even though no hatch is in evidence, being aware of what might hatch or what's been hatching can be most helpful when choosing patterns. For example, when I used to fish the Esopus Creek in the Catskills (before the New York City Department of Water Supply and the tubing goons ruined it), I knew the seasonal emergence cycle quite well. In mid-May, I found that a March Brown imitation was usually a good choice, because it was currently in season and the trout had an awareness of it.

This tactic seems to have general application across the continent. Out West, flyfishers often enjoy excellent results with imitations of the huge salmon fly during its season, even when none are on the water, or perhaps the western green drake during its time, or a hopper pattern in August. You see, trout *do* retain a consciousness, for a while, of a significant food source that was recently plentiful.

Size of fly and water conditions will govern choice of leader tippet. It is not necessary or desirable to use a very fine tippet in the sort water we are about to enter, it's a liability. Refer to the leader/fly recommendations in Chapter 3. Neither is a long leader advisable here; eight to ten feet should be plenty.

POINT OF ENTRY

Try to get into the stream at a spot that doesn't look as though it has much potential, and positions you to cast to identifiable holding lies. In this type of water, you'll be making fairly short casts, keeping as little line on the water as possible, so as to minimize the destructive effects of the current. The two main keys to success are:

1. Accuracy
2. Quality of float.

The latter refers to the behavior of the fly on the water. The most important difference between your fly and a natural is that there is a leader and line tied to yours, and the currents have something to work against. The result is that eternal bane of the dry-fly fisher: drag. Trout do not take dragging flies, with rare exceptions. Your mission is to manage a presentation that creates an illusion of detachment. This is a matter of where and how you cast and how you manipulate your tackle afterwards.

PRESENTATION

From a downstream vantage point, your casts will be upstream and/or up-and-across. The idea is to get the fly into drift lines that will take it to holding locations that you have identified. *You allow the currents to fish the fly for you.*

In certain situations, we must cast directly upstream, thereby laying the leader over the fish. Sometimes this works, but usually it's a far better practice to angle the cast, so that the leader—and where necessary, the line—fall onto the water to one side or another of a fish, or where you think there's a fish. This minimizes the chance that the leader will be immediately noticed. The key is to allow the trout to see the fly first, and focus its attention on it. Get the fish thinking, *food*. It may thus fail to notice that this morsel is attached to something, and has a sharp bit of steel hanging from its bottom.

It is very important to make the first cast count, whether presenting to a rising fish or prospecting. *Trout are more likely to take a fly the first time they see it*, provided it comes to them in a natural manner. If the fly has been presented unnaturally one or more times, with drag and all that, the trout may not believe even the best of subsequent presentations. So if you need some warmups, keep them out of the target zone. When casting to trout, fire for effect.

This is not to say that repeated casts and drifts are a no-no; quite the contrary. What I said was, don't show a trout a fly with a bad cast and then expect it to believe the good one that follows. Often it is necessary to drift a fly over a fish several or more times to stimulate the feeding impulse, or to get that absolutely perfect line of drift that draws the strike. That's fine, but each float must have enough credibility that the quarry is not alarmed or turned off.

When fishing from downstream, you have the advantage of being below the trout, and thus less noticeable. This allows shorter casts. Exactly how short is a case-by-case matter, but for our exercise, let's say twenty-five to thirty feet. The point of aim is above the target area, a spot that introduces the fly to that drift line we discussed. Try to develop sufficient line speed to cause the line and leader to fully extend in the air just above the surface. This makes the fly come to an abrupt stop, kick over and land gently.

Just how far to cast above the spot where you think the trout will take is something you have to decide, based on the circumstances that prevail. In faster, more diffused currents, a short drift is usually sufficient, and in fact, preferred. The currents tend to cover the slight commotion caused by the leader falling onto the water. The trout are used to insects quickly appearing and disappearing. Long drifts under such conditions introduce all sorts of complications. So don't cast too far upstream of these fish, you are only exacerbating your problems.

The short, "punched" type of cast also causes something else good to happen. When the line and leader straighten in the air with impetus, there is an immediate reaction, a sort of "kick-back." This produces a bit of slack: the line and leader are fully extended, but not absolutely tight or straight as they fall onto the surface. This allows the line and leader to become integrated with the currents and buffers against immediate drag. In some situations, the caster deliberately throws a lot of slack into a cast, but we'll save that lesson for the next pool.

This may sound hackneyed, but I see people violating it all the time.

Cover the holding spots nearest you first, and gradually extend your range. It is poor practice to "line" a bunch of fish and then toss them a fly. Very basic, and very important.

DRIFT MANAGEMENT

The result of an upstream cast is that the line starts drifting back towards the angler immediately. In order to keep in touch with the fly, you must deal with this, and be prepared to tighten on a fish. This is simply a matter of a controlled stripping-in of the line. This is accomplished by looping the line over the index finger, or perhaps the index and middle fingers of the rod hand and stripping in with the other hand. The rod weighs little and can be held by the unoccupied fingers.

The line can be allowed to accumulate on the water in front of or beside you. Keep it as neat as possible; you don't want any snarls to cope with if a fish takes and runs. And don't let it tangle around your legs. When the drift is completed, this line is worked back out through the guides with a few false casts.

Even if you aren't terribly happy with it, allow each presentation to drift well below the target area before picking up and casting again. One of the surest ways to put fish on their guard is to move a fly suddenly or violently, yanking it crosscurrent or ripping it off the water. You are far better off letting a misdirected cast drift, rather than to abort it. That way, you at least get a second chance.

VARYING CURRENTS

Those same deflections that provide holding spots for trout also cause variations in current flow, and often make a detached-appearing float very difficult to attain.

Let's imagine a large rock sitting in the stream in water a few feet deep. It forces a break in the currents, with a sizeable slack area below the rock. Anglers call such spots "pockets," and they are considered prime cover, because they offer the fish shelter from the currents and proximity to food supply at the same time.

Pockets differ in structure, and some are much easier to fish than others. If the rock does not protrude above the surface and there is sufficient water passing over it, there may no real problem in getting the fly to drift naturally over it and into the pocket below; the pocket is deep enough that currents can flow right over the slack water beneath. This is an ideal setup. The trout has its refuge and the angler has a fairly even flow in which to drift the fly.

Sometimes the problem with such pockets lies in identifying them, as they may be concealed by innocuous-looking surface flows. I call these hidden pockets. That's where reading water comes into play.

The tough-to-fish pockets are those where the deflection is really profound. Visualize a large boulder protruding above the surface, or perhaps one of those bridge abutments mentioned earlier. The stream goes dashing by on each side, while immediately below, the water is stopped completely, or worse, circles back upstream in a drift-wrecking swirl. Drag City!

Many anglers simply pass up such spots or make a few halfhearted casts, sigh, and move on. That's a shame. These are often the best holding spots, and it is well worth the effort to learn the various "junk" casts and sophisticated line/leader manipulations that enable contrived presentations in such situations. Essentially, the drill is to throw a lot of slack out there and try to set things up so that the currents interact against that slack while the fly floats naturally, even for just a second or two. This is a science unto itself, and we will explore it in more detail in the chapter on pocket water.

Moving

As you cover likely spots and exhaust possibilities, you will gradually work your way upstream, positioning yourself for the next target area. In doing this, try not to wade through prime holding lies. Stay in the riffles and unproductive spots as much as possible. You may intimidate a trout by wading past its lair, but that's far better than kicking the poor creature out of it. After you've gone, they forget.

Don't become a rock-hound. Earlier I commented that climbing up onto rocks is not good practice. Neither is wading up behind them into the pockets they create, to escape the current. You see, *the trout are doing the very same thing!* Of course, if you get into trouble in rough water and need respite, then your priorities change and you do whatever is required to save your body. But the idea is to not put yourself in that sort of predicament.

As you progress through a run, keep reading and rereading the water; it may be quite a bit different than it appeared from the shore. And pay attention, there may be sneaky little rises going on that weren't visible from farther away. It is amazing how inconspicuously trout can surface feed in the slack pockets behind rocks, even with racing currents close at hand.

No Strikes?

If you are convinced that you are fishing properly in good holding water, and nothing is happening, you can either enjoy the outdoors and work on your casting, or change something. That something, most likely, will be the fly. I don't advocate constant fly changes; you end up becoming great at tying knots at the expense of fishing time. On the other hand, there's little to be gained by flogging the water with something the trout are telling you they don't care for. Change flies thoughtfully, not compulsively. Consider the water; perhaps the currents are too diffused for the small fly you have on, and something larger is required. Or perhaps it's the other way around.

Consider the sky. Is it a bright, clear day? Take off that beloved Royal Wulff and go to something drab and darkly shaded: the Adams, perhaps, or a small Gray Wulff. Usually, smaller flies are better on bright days, and also, if they will float in the type of water at hand, more sparsely dressed flies.

Perhaps a change of tippet is in order—light, or lack of it, will also affect that. Again, this can be overdone. I see a lot of anglers constantly fiddling with their leaders when there's no reason for doing so. But if you're fishing 3X and nothing's happening, you may want to try 4X or 5X, particularly if you are also down-sizing your fly. And in the process, you may wish to take this opportunity to lengthen the leader a bit, if conditions appear to warrant.

Strikes!

Your fly brings some positive responses and draws strikes. The question then becomes, are you hooking fish or just moving them? If you are raising trout with any consistency and hooking few or none, something's wrong. In almost all cases, strikes that don't result in hookups are refusals; the fish was sufficiently curious to swirl at the fly, but not convinced enough to take it.

Don't be too quick to blame your reflexes. If a trout *really* wants a fly, even the most inept striker will get a hookup more often than not. It's actually hard to take the fly away from an aggressive fish. It is much more likely that either:

1. The fly isn't quite right.
2. The leader isn't quite right.
3. The drift isn't quite right.

If the drift is the culprit, you may score simply by doing a better job of presentation, using the same fly that drew the strike in the first place. Sometimes a little hidden drag, unnoticed by the angler, is enough to cause the trout to refuse or miss the fly, and it's merely a matter of making a subtle correction in the float.

If presentation is not the culprit, then you must decide whether it's fly, leader or both. A refusal is often caused by the fly being a bit too large, in which case the rule of thumb is to drop down a size. But if you are already fishing a small fly, that may not be the answer. This may dictate a reduction in tippet size, not so much because the trout sees the tippet, but because it is too heavy to allow a natural drift.

The Hatch

All of a sudden, you spot a rise, then another, and several more. A fortuitous occurrence; there's nothing like casting to surface-feeding fish! One of the most exciting happenings in all of angling is to be fishing a piece of water futilely, ready to swear there isn't a fish in it, and suddenly have it erupt with rising trout.

The first order of business is to identify the cause. Look for insects, and if you see some, try to follow their drift into good holding spots and places where you have seen rises. If you actually see a fish take a floating fly, you're in business. Now all that's required is to match the hatch and get your fly over the feeding trout without drag.

The Pool Proper

Hatch time is often the right time to consider a move to the big pool below. While it generally isn't wise to leave rising trout, there may well be enhanced opportunities in slower water, where trout have an easier time rising to floating insects. You look downstream, and sure enough, fish are rising throughout the pool. You move in that direction.

This is quite a different setup: slower, calmer water, little or no visible structure, harder-to-read drift lines. So before we jump into this pool and start flailing away, it is well that we understand some things about pools and how the residents behave.

There are several phenomena that contribute to making a pool:

1. Reduced gradient.
2. Increased depth.
3. Increased width.
4. Altered structure.

Each and all of these may be present in a given pool. Individually and collectively, their main effect is to slow the current.

Like fast runs, pools vary a great deal, but they do have certain classic characteristics. The pool at hand features a head, where the run from above flows in, then slows and becomes more pacific. There follows a long, slow section, then a tail, where the currents gather themselves for the riffle below.

Our pool is actually a model of a famous pool on a renowned river, both of which will remain nameless. Look at the graphics; they depict the architecture of this piece of water. Note the contours of the stream-bed, the shape from overhead and the asymmetrical cross section. What we have here is a giant, lopsided bath tub.

As described previously, the pool has a shallow side and a deep side. The shallow side is bordered by a road. The deep side follows the base of a very steep hillside. An old abandoned railroad bed is cut into this hillside, about twenty feet above the water line, where one can walk, sit, and study the scene below. This railroad bed plays an important role in the fishing of this pool, but often it is ignored for the simple reason that many anglers are lazy and would rather take the less strenuous approach.

There are a number of ways to fish this pool, some good and some not. On any clement weekend, one may observe plenty of both going on. The ease of access from the road side lures many casual fly fishers, some of whom are still early on the learning curve. They make a lot of mistakes. The trout, mostly carry-overs from previous stockings, are people-conditioned and quite tolerant, but not forgiving. Fish, you may. Catch, you well may not.

THE HEAD, AND SEAMS

This is where the run we have been fishing enters the main pool. There is still a fair amount of current in the middle, but to each side, the river widens and slows. There is a moderate bend here that also contributes some structure, creating a large slack area on the road side. There would be lots of trout living in that part of the pool if it weren't that people insist on wading in there and scaring them out. Once in a while, usually early in the morning, I find this area undisturbed, and sure enough, the trout have moved back in—but that doesn't last long.

Wherever faster and slower currents lie adjacent to each other, there is a narrow strip of "transition" water, that I like to call a "seam." Seams are of great importance, because they are prime feeding lanes; the faster current brings the food, while the slower water lets the trout hold in comfort.

Seams can be very narrow where the disparity in currents is abrupt and profound, or wide where the transition is more gradual. Usually there are two seams, one on each side of the main current, except where the pool is on a sharp bend, and the faster current hugs one bank.

As mentioned, insects are drifting down from the run above. Many of them slip off to the side and into the seams, where the trout are lined up for an easy meal. At such times, rises in and along the edges of the seam will be in evidence. They are more or less obvious, depending on several factors. Sometimes the rises are delicate and hard to spot; trout don't normally spend more energy taking food than is necessary. But at other times the rises may be vigorous, indicating that the trout are excited. This can be brought on by:

1. Heavy emergences of larger insects.
2. The insects' behavior—fluttering on the surface, trying to fly away.
3. Ideal water temperature and oxygen level—the trout feel exuberant.
4. Competitive instincts towards other trout feeding close by.

Positioning

The ideal way to fish a seam is to stand in the slow or slack water and cast across and up, dropping the dry onto the seam above a rising fish. Exact position and casting angle are governed by the nuances of the currents. In cases where there is a drastic difference in current speeds—a narrow seam—you may have to cast the line and leader directly up the drift line, in order to avoid drag.

Think that over; it is one of the eternal tenets of dry-fly fishing. Unless you are employing some type of variant cast or line management trick, *a drag-free float depends on the fly, leader and line moving at the same speed.* As we go along, we shall see how this influences our presentations on other types of water.

When casting into a seam from an angle, the tendency of the current is to move the fly faster than the leader and line, which is lying in slack water. What happens then is that the leader retards the drift speed of the fly, causing reverse drag. Whether upstream or down, drag is drag, and it will defeat you unless it is counteracted. Let's explore ways to do just that.

THE "S" CAST

This technique is one of the oldest and easiest methods of compensating for drag. Execution is very simple; one merely waggles the rod from side to side as the forward cast straightens, causing it to fall onto the surface in an "S" pattern. This forces the faster current to work against slack, rather than a tight line and leader. The effect is to extend the duration of the drag-free drift. This type of cast takes a little practice, but not a whole lot, even a beginner can learn it quickly.

Waggling the rod laterally during the cast configures the line in snakelike wriggles on the water.

THE "STOP" CAST

This is another simple technique for putting some slack into a cast. You will recall that in fishing the run, we discussed letting the forward cast straighten forcefully in the air, so that it kicked back a little as it landed. The stop cast is simply that technique with more emphasis. Here's how it's done; as the forward cast straightens, bring the rod back and upwards, almost as though you were beginning another back cast. The difference is that you stop when the rod is approximately vertical. This creates a counterforce, the effect of which is two-fold:

1. The fly kicks over and lands first.
2. Some slack in the form of Ss occurs in line and leader, in a manner similar to the S cast.

The variations of this technique are practical infinite; the amount of force exerted and the amount of rod movement affect the degree of slack obtained. It does require some practice, but it is the kind of practice one can do astream, while actually fishing. During slow periods when nothing's hatching, pick a challenging stretch of water and see how good a drift you can create, implementing these casting variations.

The "stop" cast. As the line is about to straighten in the air, the rod is brought back and up, which results in a slack cast falling onto the water.

THE MAIN POOL

Below the head, the pool widens, flattens and slows even more. This is leisurely water, with little or no visible structure. There may be plenty of structure along the streambed, but because of the depth and slowness of the currents, it does not effect the surface. This makes the water difficult to read, which is one of the reasons flat pools are not good places for fishing blind—one simply can't tell precisely where a trout may be holding. Generally, we save the slow pools for hatch or spinner fall time.

Except along the banks, the flow is more-or-less even across the pool. Still, there is almost always some disparity. Very few stretches of water have such an even flow that one can cast directly across and just let everything drift along drag-free.

Typically, what we encounter is slightly faster current in the center; the main current. Because the water is much more gentle, trout are inclined to feed all over this area, even in the main current. These slow-water trout behave differently than do their relatives who reside in faster currents. They can afford to take their time and examine their food more closely, for there's no hurry.

SLOW-WATER RISES

The trout in faster runs, riffles and pockets tend to be opportunists. They have to be; an insect suddenly appears, and just as suddenly is gone. In slow water, the trout see insects coming from much farther and can observe them for a longer period of time. They also get a better look at other things above them: lines, leaders, us. This implies a much more critical set of circumstances.

Slow-pool trout aren't slaves to their lie, they can move about with little effort. They may move to one side or another to take a morsel that looks good to them, and they may drift with a fly, taking their own sweet time to commit. When this is happening, the angler must be aware that the taking point where the rise is seen may be far downstream of a trout's holding spot. Failure to appreciate and allow for this results in presenting the fly below the fish.

Remember the railroad bed? One of its greatest values is as an observation post. It affords a high vantage point from which one may observe the goings-on in the pool below while remaining inconspicuous. If conditions are right, what you will see is trout rising slowly toward the surface, drifting with the current, looking over a fly, finally taking it, then swimming back upstream to where the sequence began. This can be a revelation.

Armed with this knowledge, the angler is now faced with the task of

The main section of the pool.

making the fly drift naturally for a long ways while casting across currents of varying speeds. The classic setup, one most frequently encountered, is casting across the main current to trout feeding on the far side of it. There may be other problems to worry about, but let's tackle this one first.

THE REACH CAST

In his writings and teachings, Lefty Kreh reveals to the angling world the following gem: "The fly line follows the rod in the direction in which the rod tip was moving when it stopped." People with Lefty's talent—and there aren't many of them—can make lines do all kinds of tricks. The average good caster—and I place myself in that category—can employ these dynamics to make better presentations. The reach cast is an example.

Here's how it's done; the forward cast is shooting out across the pool. Late in its development, but before it straightens, the caster moves the rod tip in an upstream direction, either across the body or to the casting-arm side, depending on which way the current is flowing. This causes the portion of the line nearest the rod tip to be deployed in something of an upstream curve. This in effect creates a buffer; an upstream "belly" of line that lies across the main current, which allows for a longer drag-free float.

The "reach" cast. As the line straightens above the water, the angler extends the casting arm upstream, effecting an upstream curve which mitigates against drag.

MENDING LINE

This enormously important maneuver is a natural addendum to the technique learned in the reach cast. That upstream belly won't last forever, quite probably not long enough to enable you to fish out the drift the way you wish. If a mid-drift correction isn't made, the fly will be dragged cross current at the most disadvantageous moment, just when the trout drifting beneath it is about to suck it in. That will blow the deal every time.

The mend is simply a matter of throwing another upstream belly into the line as it is drifting. The move is quite similar to that of the reach cast, except that you must pick part of the line up off the surface. The leader, and preferably, a portion of the front end of the line remains in place on the water. The surface tension anchors one end while the caster moves the rest.

Think of two kids playing jump-rope. If one is to do the jumping, that leaves the other kid to work the rope. To accomplish this, the kid ties the end of the rope to a tree or something. That's essentially the way the mend works.

As a fly fisher, you are going to spend the rest of your life mending line, and it will become almost second nature. The mend can be repeated during the course of a drift, as required. It can also be executed as soon as the line lands on the water, to get the drift off to a good start. The idea is to make the mend before you desperately need it, at a point where it won't disturb trout in the area.

SUNLIGHT AND SHADE

The dry-fly fisher has few enemies that are the equal of bright sunlight. This is true in all types of water, but in calm pools, it is worse. Trout do not like bright light. They know it exposes them to those nasty ospreys and kingfishers up there, and it also bothers their vision, because they have no eyelids and can't blink. Think how you'd feel if you couldn't blink your eyes under such conditions.

Even so, the lure of plentiful food will get the trout going on sunny days, and the angler must cope with the problems this presents, such as:

1. The leader is much more conspicuous on the water.
2. The movement of the line in the air may be noticeable.
3. Ditto the rod and reel during casting.
4. The trout sees objects outside the water better, including us.
5. The fish are just plain spooky, for reasons mentioned.

Mending line. As the current begins to induce a downstream curve in the drifting line, the angler flips the "belly" of the line upstream, thus avoiding drag. To execute this, the leader and the front end of the line must remain on the water, so that the angler has something to work against. The motion is very much like that shown in the reach cast.

And let me tell you something else; insects don't like light very much, either. They are instinctively aware of birds, and how lethal they can be when visibility is good. That's why many hatches come off in late evening and on dark days. Some species have evolved as nocturnal emergers because their large size and slow flight make them an easy target, the huge *Hexagenias* of Michigan being a perfect example.

But there are lots of flies that do come off in the daytime when the sun is beating down. Nature has provided for their survival through proliferation; the birds can't eat them all, even with the help of the fish. And so the trout feed; skittishly, to be sure, but they do feed.

Here are several hints for making the best of bright-day fishing:

1. Wear drab clothing, hats in particular.
2. Use a fly line with a dull finish. This is even more important than the specific color. It's line flash during casting that scares fish. But avoid "hot" colors; they are okay for some things, but not for casting over a flat pool on a sunny day.
3. Avoid buying the flashiest reel in the store. Few people think about this. Reel manufacturers want their products to have eye appeal, and they don't consider that a shiny finish gives off blinding flashes on bright days that are visible for half a mile or more. There *are* choices in this respect.
4. Stay low and move deliberately.
5. Avoid false casting over trout, it makes them very nervous. Try to do your false casting off to the side.

Okay, you can't change the weather, but you can plan around it and make adaptations. Unless you have a lot of energy and enthusiasm to spare, or have no other time to go fishing, I would suggest avoiding the bright part of the day. Tie some flies, fix up your leaders, clean your fly lines, take a nap, and give it your best shot in morning and evening.

That's a general statement. In spring and fall, many important insects are daytime emergers: the Hendricksons in the East and Midwest, the Pale Morning Duns and various Baetis in the West. Their appearance can offset the negative effects of sunlight. These are the sort of things it's good to know.

It is also of great value to become intimately familiar with the terrain surrounding the rivers you fish. Mountains, hills, high banks, even large shade trees can make a world of difference. Many rivers have morning and evening pools, imposed by sources of shade and their position in relation to the sun. You can optimize your day astream by playing the follow-the-shade game.

THE DEEP BANK

Take another look at the cross-section drawing and note again the asymmetry of our pool. The deep side, beneath the steep bank and the old railroad is virtually impossible to fish from the road side. It's a very long cast across varied currents, and one can't wade in the middle. But this is actually the best holding water in the entire pool. Depth and large boulders provide ideal lies. Food is plentiful and easy to get. The high bank retards the current and provides shade. In summer, underground springs on the hillside send cooling flows that keep the trout healthy and happy. All is wonderful, except for one thing—it's a miserable place to try to fish.

But it's worth the effort, and there are ways to go about it. Except in periods of high water, one can wade upstream from the tail of the pool for quite a distance before the water gets too deep, so that's a viable option. It means casting directly up and over the fish, but you're stuck with that anyway, because of the currents. Of course, you fish your way up.

The unwadable portion can be fished after a fashion from the bank; there's just enough room to stand on the boulders. This places the angler above the trout. Not the best situation—but the bank offers enough camouflage that you aren't silhouetted against the sky.

In this particular pool, left-handers have a decided advantage, because their casting arms are on the stream side. Right-handers either have to learn to switch over or master the crossbody cast, which was my answer. Fortunately, long casts aren't required here, and the seldom-fished-for trout are blessedly free-rising.

THE TAIL

In some pools, the tail has little to offer, being shallow and lacking in structure. This pool, however, is different. As the drawing shows, the water stays fairly deep almost to the very end, then the bottom slopes up sharply and the water runs out to form the long riffle below.

Where such a contour exists, the mass of earth at the end creates a large area of slow water; in effect, a hydraulic cushion. Fish can exist and feed quite comfortably here. During periods of high water, especially in the spring, this can be one of the better holding spots in the pool.

The main problem that is encountered in this sort of situation is speed of current. If one tries to stand in the riffle below and cast upstream to fish in the tail of the pool, the fast-moving water will pull on the line and drag the fly. Water usually accelerates as it leaves a pool, and that makes for a tough situation when fishing from downstream.

There are two other options: you can present the fly from the side or possibly from above. The latter requires positioning oneself upstream of the fish without scaring them and making slack casts downstream. Which might be more productive is a case-by-case matter. Personally, I rather like downstream dry-fly fishing. We will explore this method further as we go on.

8

Riffles, Pocket Water, and Small Creeks

The Riffle

While riffles generally don't amount to much, some are amazingly rich and productive, loaded with insect life, and able to hold trout at all times, except perhaps in periods of low water. And even those that don't have adequate structure to hold resident fish can come alive when a heavy hatch lures hungry trout into the thin, fast water to gorge themselves.

Structure

Riffles are typified by a steeper gradient, faster and shallower water and lack of heavy structure. Some have so little structure that even small trout can find no sanctuary, but remember; it doesn't take much of a rock to create a pocket in which a fish can hold. In other words, there are riffles and there are riffles.

This is where reading water comes into play. Don't get into the habit of considering all riffles as merely places to wade up or down to the next pool. Look them over, especially on darker days, when trout aren't so paranoid. Try an attractor fly in the fishy-looking spots. You may be pleasantly surprised by the results.

A very fishy-looking riffle, with lots of character and structure, and a pocket here and there.

BEHAVIOR

Riffle fish tend to be opportunists. Food passes by quickly; vision is illusory and imprecise, characterized by fleeting, distorted images. It's a matter of eat it now or lose it forever.

In a no-hatch situation, this type of water is ideal for the nonspecific fly: the Wulff, the Variant, the Irresistible, the Humpy, whatever. The key characteristic of an effective riffle fly is flotation; high-riding, effervescent, bouncy, alive. We want the fly to dance along on the currents.

Strikes are sudden in this type of water, and one must be ready. A boil beneath a fly indicates interest, and usually the thing to do is to rest that fish for a few moments, let it settle down, then offer the same fly again, taking care to get the best possible drift. Remember that structure is conservative here, so accuracy is important. Presentation and casting problems are lessened by the fact that it is seldom necessary to use a long leader and fine tippet in riffle fishing.

If the fly is refused on subsequent presentations, it's a good idea to switch. Tie on something similar, perhaps a size smaller. If you were fishing a 3X tippet, go to 4X. Give the fish a good rest, and make the first cast with the new fly count.

POSITIONING

A typical riffle is approached from below, and fished upstream. There is the possibility that the nature of the currents may facilitate fishing from either side. Under certain circumstances, it is even possible to fish a riffle from above. I'll touch on that.

It should be kept in mind that in shallow water, trout are particularly skittish about what might come down on them from above, so the angler must avoid being seen. Usually, the best way is to fish upstream, but if the particular riffle sets up well for crosscurrent fishing, that's okay. Just be sure to maintain a low silhouette, and try to keep the sun behind you. Remember that the trout can't blink its eye or dilate the pupil. Make the fish look into the source of light.

A less provocative-looking riffle, with minimal structure. Still, it can be productive under certain circumstances.

Something to watch out for when fishing up a riffle is downstream drag, where the current below the target area is a little faster than that in the target area itself. You cast, and the line drops onto the water. The more rapid current nearest you pulls the leader and fly downstream.

There are several ways to prevent this. One is to alter slightly the direction of the cast, dropping the line at a moderate angle, rather than directly upstream, allowing it to fall in slower sidecurrents. Another is to simply not wade into that sort of position; but perhaps it's the ideal location, except for that one problem. In that case, what you may be able to do is raise the rod and keep the line up off the water. Since we normally don't fish a long line in a riffle, this may be feasible This is one of the main reasons I like long fly rods; they enable more effective line management in situations such as these.

I mentioned that sometimes a presentation in a riffle may be made from upstream. Why would one want to do this, and how?

Envision this situation. You have waded a short ways up a riffle, or perhaps you have entered it in the middle, rather than from the very bottom. A trout begins to feed below you. Yes, this will happen, even though you may have walked through the area just moments earlier. Food makes trout forget in a hurry.

Rather than walk all the way around and come up on the trout from downstream, you may simply throw a slack cast directly above the rise and let a little line slip through the guides to prevent immediate drag. I have found this a most effective technique. The one liability is that fish rising to this sort of a presentation are often difficult to hook, because the act of setting the hook may yank the fly right out of the fish's mouth. In faster currents, this usually isn't so serious a problem, because of the vigor with which the trout takes the fly. On quiet pools, it can be most frustrating.

I would advise that when you do hook a fish on a downstream cast, you try to get below it right away. In the case of small trout, this may not be necessary; you can usually just sort of skid them upstream. In the case of larger fish—those you may want to get into the net for a brief show-off to nearby anglers—playing from an upstream position will result in frequent unhookings.

RIFFLE HATCHES

Many aquatic insects require briskly moving currents for their existence. Such water holds more oxygen, and the currents passing through the insect's gills facilitate a form of breathing. When these insects emerge, a large supply of food becomes available to the trout. Under these conditions, trout not resident to the riffle may move up from more moderate currents below, in order to intercept the insects before they can take wing.

A riffle hatch can be exciting. Rise forms are often slashing and incisive, the get-it-before-it-escapes syndrome. Trout tend to leap in the shallow water, which is always lots of fun; however, the commotion of a trout falling back into the water can spook those nearby. Therefore, if you can manage it, try to lead a hooked fish out of the target area as soon as possible.

Some evening, when standing in a riffle, you may find yourself inundated by spinners returning to oviposit. Usually, the drill is to move downstream to quieter waters. The insects may fall spent on the riffle, but that isn't where the trout want to take them. They much prefer to suck them in at leisure in the pool below.

Pocket Water

We touched on this type of structure when fishing the run above our classic pool in a previous chapter. My definition of pocket water, as opposed to a run, is that it is virtually *all* pockets, instead of just a few of them located at random in a stretch of water.

Such water can be physically taxing as well as technically demanding. The currents between the pockets can be very swift, and wading treacherous, requiring prudence and caution. But the results may be well worth the effort. Heavily-structured pockets offer trout cover and food supply in abundance. Also, the adventurous angler may avoid the crowds by opting to fish more intimidating parts of the stream.

Pocket water is generally quite difficult to fish, because everything is broken up into pieces, currents are wildly diverse, and it is most difficult to get any appreciable drift. The thing to keep in mind is that trout residing in pockets see natural insects in the same manner they do the artificials we present to them: suddenly and briefly. Therefor, it may not be necessary to obtain much of a drift at all.

Another factor in our favor is that heavy pocket water interferes with the trout's ability to see and "hear" approaching anglers. I use quotes around the term "hear," because trout don't have exterior ears with which to actually hear sounds the way we do. Instead, they have inner ears and acute sensory nerves along the lateral line that enable them to detect vibrations. In quiet waters, even minor vibrations can be detected. Rough currents muffle the sounds of our approach and make us less noticeable from a visual standpoint as well.

Classic pocket water.

This large midstream rock creates two pockets: one above and one below.

POSITIONING

The variety and complexity of pocket-water configurations makes it difficult to specify one approach that will apply to all situations. Fishing such water is usually an upstream proposition; we move to the pocket from below and cast up into it. But that's not always the best procedure. Sometimes the layout of the stream makes it easier to get at the pocket from one side or the other.

One thing that is highly desirable, and often next to impossible, is to position oneself so that there is no disparity in current speed between where the fly will fall onto the water and where the line is held off the surface by the tip of the rod. The reason, obviously, is to eliminate that hated downstream drag that was described in the riffle section. But few pockets are so structured, unless they are very large and actually comprise a small pool that you and the cast can all fit into.

Let's say the angler finds himself or herself standing in the lower end of the pocket, or in faster water below it. Because of its interaction with the structure that creates the pocket, the current is swirly and diffuse. Whirlpools and eddies abound, yet somehow we must get a fly to appear detached and natural in this snake pit.

READING A POCKET

Pockets vary considerably, but there are a few things that seem to be common to most of them. Let's look at a typical configuration. There is the large rock or boulder at the head, immediately below which is the pocket proper, a piece of obstructed water that just sort of jiggles around and doesn't really go anywhere. In some cases, it is almost dead calm.

Below that, the currents from either side start to come back together. The beginning of this part of the pocket is usually the hot spot, even more so than the slack section. There is plenty of protection from the main current, yet there is enough current to keep the trout happy, well balanced and well oxygenated. Trout may rush into the calm area to grab a fly, but usually they hold where the two seams of current begin to rejoin. If sufficient space exists, there may be several of them there.

To this point, we have been considering only the lower pocket; the one below the obstruction. Quite often, there is another one immediately in front of the obstruction; call it a frontal pocket. It is caused by the pressure of the water flowing against the obstruction, which retards the current and creates a sort of hydraulic cushion.

The frontal pocket is often overlooked by the uninitiated. The lower pocket literally screams *trout!*, and demands the angler's full attention

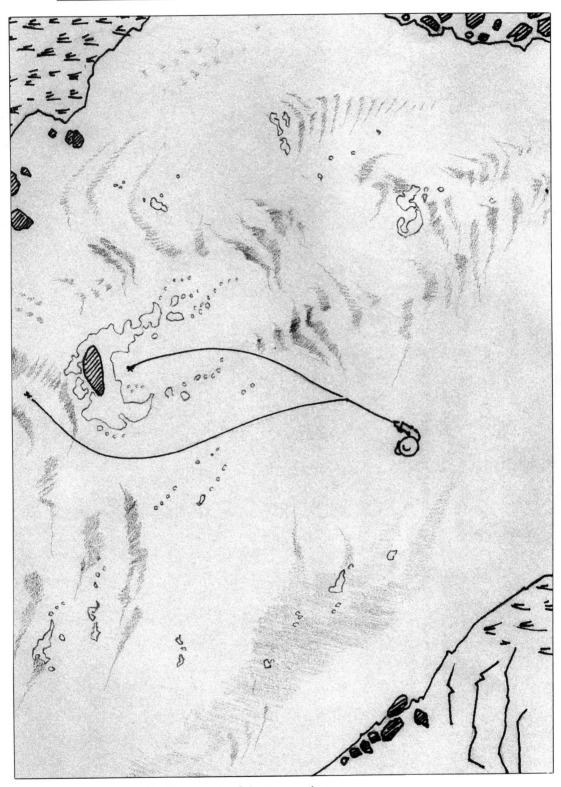

An angler presenting a dry fly to each of the two pockets.

Pocket water of a different character. The numbered solid lines represent casts. The lettered broken lines show potential drifts that would carry a fly into a likely holding area.

and effort. But let me tell you; I have risen *so* many beautiful trout in frontal pockets, and they are easier to fish, because the currents carry the fly directly to where the fish is positioned, with little or no interference. It's about as close as one comes to a free lunch in this game.

Trout do rise in pockets, which of course is very much to our benefit, for we can then see where the trout is taking its food, and perhaps what that food looks like. When this occurs, part of the reading process is done for us. What remains is the water read, where we determine how to present to fish that have shown themselves. Rises in pockets can range from vigorous to sneaky, depending on the idiosyncrasies of the currents. Where there is a dead calm or very slow spot, rise forms are apt to be subtle, so be observant, and don't start flailing away until you've taken a moment to see if anything interesting is going on.

Presentation

Unless the pocket in question is a rare easy-to-fish one, you'll be forced to make one "garbage" cast after another. A short leader is called for: eight feet, maybe seven, perhaps even as little as six, when the pockets are small. This is an aid both to casting and presentation. Because casts are so short, it is difficult to get enough line weight moving in the air to load the rod and generate power. The shorter the leader, the greater the amount of line that can be brought into play; it is far easier to cast line than leader. As for presentation, a short leader turns over much more readily than does a long one.

This is the domain of the bird's-nest leader. Several techniques have been presented that enable a slack deployment of the leader, rather than a straight-line deployment. You'll get plenty of chances to practice them in pocket-water dry-fly fishing. You will work out your own style of throwing slack onto the water. The thing is to forget classic technique and simply make whatever alterations are necessary to cause the leader to fall in a semiorganized bunch, so that the fly can sit for a moment without anything pulling at it—except, perhaps, a deluded trout.

Small Freestone Streams

The techniques for fishing the dry fly in small mountain brooks are very similar to those for fishing pocket water. Indeed, the typical pool in such a stream isn't much more than a pocket.

Cramped quarters, small target areas, and brief floats demand tackle considerations similar to those of pockets: weight-forward lines and short leaders. In addition, a shorter, faster-action rod is preferred, as trees and bushes limit casting room. I have rods as short as six feet, but in such an environment my preference is for a seven-footer for a three- or four-weight line.

APPROACH AND PRESENTATION

These are the most critical considerations of all. Trout in small streams have minimal cover, and they know it. They are nervous to the extreme and very intolerant of movement above. Therefore, the keys are: stay low, and stay downstream. I can think of very few situations where a small stream sets up for anything other than up-and-over presentations. In some cases it is advisable to kneel in the riffle below a little pool while casting up into it.

Scaring the trout is sometimes unavoidable. In such cases, patience will carry the day. Sit down below the pool, out of sight, and wait it out. After a while they forget. Give the fish a chance to settle back into their normal routine. If they were rising when you spooked them, allow them to resume their feeding rhythm. Then choose a fish and make the first cast count.

In riffles and pocket water, we learned that working progressively upstream and casting to the lowermost trout is the usual procedure. This may also be true on small creeks, but there are exceptions. The most common is where a larger trout is identified in a pool, and the angler opts to try for it, to the exclusion of any others. Then, you simply set up to make your Class A cast to that fish. If there is a way to do this without scaring the others, by all means do so. Otherwise, just go for it.

Unless a hatch is in progress, small-creek trout are seldom selective. Most of these streams have limited insect life, and the fish are always hungry and quite competitive for food. General flies, such as the Adams, work great here, in sizes 12 to 16. Caddis imitations usually produce well, as do terrestrials: ants, beetles, small hoppers and crickets.

Although fishing these little creeks can tax one's patience, thanks to overhanging trees, bushes and such, it can also be a most rewarding undertaking. Many go virtually unfished; they don't get written up in the magazines. One can fish in peace and solitude for wild trout, which are sometimes of surprising size.

If you become a small-stream addict, I counsel you to be secretive, especially with worm-fishers and the like. A skilled bait fisher can clean out a small creek in no time. A word to the wise.

A very fishable small freestone stream. Absence of trees along the bank abet casting, but make a low profile mandatory.

The Slow, Flat Pool

WE ARE ABOUT TO LOOK AT A WATER TYPE THAT CAN BE AGONIZINGLY difficult to fish, but highly rewarding. I refer to the very slow pool that has little or no visible structure or character. This is much flatter and slower than the one we examined in the chapter that dealt with the classic pool; this is a *real frog pond!*

These pools all have one thing in common—if there isn't something happening that causes the trout to rise, one wouldn't believe there's a fish in the place. Unless trout are feeding visibly, I wouldn't even think of fishing such water. Every part of the pool looks exactly the same. There are no deflections, no identifiable targets. In repose, these pools are about as interesting as a blackboard with nothing written on it.

So why would trout take up residence in the first place? The answer is: easy livin'. Complex structure is replaced by two things; depth and lack of current. If the water is slow enough and deep enough, structure is not essential.

Consider that the slowest currents in a pool are at the bottom. The streambed, even if it is a virtual sidewalk, has the effect of retarding the current, dragging on it, slowing it down. Thus, the least little deflection becomes a viable holding lie. Depth provides cover from above. There is a limit to how deep an osprey or kingfisher can see a fish, let alone catch it. The trout blissfully lie on the bottom in unconcerned comfort.

Opposite: Some very large and cerebral trout live in this placid, terrifying pool. About the only thing that helps the angler is the bushy foliage along each bank, which breaks up his silhouette.

The one piece of structure that is sometimes present in such pools, and it can be of enormous importance, is a deep bank, or even two of them. Banks have the same retarding effect on water flows that streambeds do. They also offer trout something of great value: near-absolute security from one side. And the holding water adjacent to shore affords access to a terrestrial food supply as well.

So, we fly fishers do have a few things going for us in such environs. But let us not minimize the problems, which are:

1. The least little disturbance, especially from overhead, will almost surely spook the fish something fierce, and it is impossible to lay a cast on the water without creating *some* disturbance.
2. Even with deep-cut banks, we are never sure where the fish are holding.
3. Trout see everything all too clearly in this type of water.
4. Sounds and vibrations are easily detectable.
5. Ripples caused by wading frighten the fish.
6. The trout may not be ready to feed, in which case we are whipping a dead horse.

Sounds horrible, yes? But down come a few bugs, and the trout move into their feeding positions and begin to focus on the insects. As the emergence or spinner fall intensifies, the trout become more and more engrossed in surface feeding, and less and less cautious. At such times, they are vulnerable to the dry fly.

APPROACH AND POSITIONING

Even with the trout rising aggressively to a good hatch, entering the water and getting into position for presentations is a demanding chore. Those waves we create when wading transmit a take-cover alarm, and trout will instantly abandon the best of feeding situations if so spooked.

In large pools, it may be feasible to enter from one side or the other, rather than from the tail. Sometimes these pools are long, and the lower portion is thin, waste water. Wading upstream through all that is tedious and increases the chances of making waves during the approach. In many cases, however, trout are feeding on both sides. It's bad practice to frighten these fish, even if they are small ones we aren't interested in, because their scurrying about can alarm other fish in the pool. Under those circumstances, you will probably want to enter from downstream.

Approaching from downstream does have a couple of advantages. It places the angler below the trout, where he or she is less likely to be seen, and waves resulting from wading do not travel upstream as readily as

A slow meadow stretch with more forgiving currents. However, the lack of bankside foliage leaves one naked against the skyline.

they do down or across. In any event, the idea is to get into casting position unnoticed. The ideal position allows the cast to be angled; it is a very tough proposition to cast directly up and over rising trout in flat water.

The downstream presentation discussed in the riffles chapter is often a successful ploy here, either directly down, or down-and-across. In fact, this is sometimes the best way to fish a slow pool. The deciding factor is whether or not the trout will tolerate someone being upstream of them. This is to some extent a matter of distance, but is also influenced by the angler's deportment. This is a time for great stealth.

As for the downstream technique, it is essentially the same in slow pools as for riffle fishing. There is a problem, however, that is considerably more persistent: hooking the fish. We'll examine this in just a bit.

There are times when a direct upstream presentation is all that's available, and we simply have to deal with it. In such cases, a long leader and fine tippet are called for. It also may be helpful to say a silent prayer for cloud cover, a bountiful hatch and a little breeze to break up the surface. Wind can be a valuable ally under certain conditions. We all hate what it does to our casts, but a ripple on the water can make all the difference in the world with presentations, and how trout respond. I've seen people driven off a stream by wind, when actually the fishing was great. Don't be intimidated; learn to cast in windy conditions.

WIND CASTING

First, a few tackle considerations. I recommend a somewhat shorter rod. I like to use a nine foot rod, but in the wind, I much prefer an eight-footer. In fact, I just purchased an eight-foot, three-weight for just this purpose.

A sedate rise in a languid pool.

The best type of line for wind casting is a forward taper; double tapers don't have as much belly out front to drive into the breeze. It is also a good idea to shorten the leader; with wind disturbing the surface, an extremely long leader is more of a hindrance than a help. This is a case-by-case deal, so I'll refrain from setting forth any specific prescriptions.

For the moment, let's assume we have a head wind. Insofar as technique is concerned, it is important to keep the line low. There's less wind down near the surface of the water, and the tighter a loop, the better the aerodynamics. Don't cast any farther than is necessary. Let the wind help develop a fast-moving back cast, and make a forceful, driving stroke on the forward cast. Don't try to finesse anything.

The same instructions apply with a tail wind: low line position, tight loop. Here, it is advisable to exert additional force on the back cast, so that the wind doesn't "stack" the line. Be very attentive to timing. The wind will seek to prevent the back cast from straightening as it normally would, and that nice, reassuring feeling that's transmitted when it's time to execute the forward cast may be missing. Rather than lose the momentum of the back cast, it's better to begin the forward cast early, the instant you sense that the back cast is about to die.

One last thought: wind is often gusty, rather than steady. Be patient, and see if it's possible to time your casts between gusts.

FEEDING BEHAVIOR

I mentioned earlier that trout in slow currents tend to drift with a fly and extend their decision-making time frame. In very slow pools, this is true in spades. Such behavior is a surface-feeding ritual, and of great concern to the dry-fly fisher. When trout are nymphing, they usually take the insect as it comes to them, rather than drift and inspect it.

It is common to see trout lying in the current, just beneath the surface, taking food as it comes by. This requires little effort, and is easier for the fish than returning to a deep lie after each take, then having to come all the way up again seconds later. It may be that these trout are taking nymphs or emerging forms, and little or nothing on the surface; the rise forms should tell you. But even when they are nymphing, trout can often be brought to a dry fly when they are holding in that sort of feeding position.

When casting over fish in this sort of situation, you may notice that one or more of the fish you've been presenting to have disappeared. Don't be too quick to castigate yourself for putting them down. What often happens is that the current, slow as it is, tires them a bit, and they go below for a breather. Wait a bit; they'll be back.

When the food supply is more or less intermittent, trout are not inclined to hold in high subsurface positions, yet rises may be seen anyway. This is directly attributable to the slow current. Trout can come up from the bottom and take a fly with very little effort, a favorable energy-for-calories exchange. Give these fish a chance; cast above the rise forms and allow them to see the fly well upstream, so they may drift up to it at their own pace.

The ease with which trout take food can affect hook engagement. A trout takes a floating fly by sucking in a bit of water, which is expelled through the gills. The slower the current, the more gentle the action. Just before the actual take, the trout loses sight of the fly; it is too close to the fish to be in its field of vision. This explains why trout often take with a rolling action, and are hooked in the corner of the mouth; the fish are trying to keep the fly in sight as long as possible. But to engulf the fly, the trout depends on a predetermined course of interception and that little sip of water.

This can create vexing problems when downstream presentations are the order of the day. The fish exerts so little effort (why should it try harder, just to accommodate us?) that the artificial fly, slightly restrained by the leader, doesn't actually make it into the trout's mouth. We see the rise, attempt to set the hook, and come up with nothing. The sipping rainbows of the Henry's Fork were about as troublesome in this respect as any trout in my experience.

All one can do is try for the best attainable drift, with just a bit of slack in the tippet, so that the fly isn't kept from being drawn in. Sometimes, if the miss is clean and the trout doesn't feel the hook, it will keep right on feeding, thinking it simply missed a bite. With due care, we may get a second chance.

We shall leave the slow pools with this reminder: choose your flies with a discriminating eye. No bushy, heavily dressed flies here. Masses of fur and thick ruffs of hackle are not required for flotation, and can only hurt your chances. Minimalism is the key.

An interesting situation. The wing deflector, installed for stream improvement purposes, has created a slow pool out of a riffle.

Spring Creeks

IF AN ANGEL WERE TO COME DOWN FROM ABOVE AND SAY TO ME, "Listen; we've decided you can fish every day for the rest of your life, but only one way, and on one kind of water. What's your choice?," I'd reply without hesitation, "I'll take dry-fly fishing on a spring creek."

The only trouble with spring creeks is that there aren't nearly enough of them. Montana, Idaho and northwestern Wyoming have a fair number. There are some in the Midwest, particularly in Wisconsin. These are mostly quite small, but rich in aquatic life. The limestone streams of Pennsylvania, such as the Letort, the Big Spring and the Falling Springs are spring creeks. There are a few small ones in western New York State. I'm told there are also some in Maryland, and in Maine. And of course, the British chalk streams, as they are called, are spring creeks.

What makes a spring creek a spring creek? Would you believe, a spring! Their origin is spontaneous. These unique streams bubble up out of the earth, as Athena sprang fully grown and armed from the brow of Zeus. Instant trout stream.

Spring creeks are generally found running through flat lands where the aquifer is close to the surface. True, there are many throughout the Rockies, but they don't run down out of the mountains, as freestone streams do. The two famous spring creeks in Montana's Paradise Valley—Nelson's and Armstrong's—are typical. They gush from the rich meadows that border the majestic Yellowstone. The mountains on either side provide a scenic backdrop.

A Montana classic: Nelson's Spring Creek, a tributary of the Yellowstone in the Paradise Valley near Livingston.

Most true spring creeks are quite short. The two just mentioned are only a few miles long, then they flow into the Yellowstone. Others which have both spring-creek and freestone-stream characteristics are longer. The Yellow Breeches in southern Pennsylvania is a good example of such a stream. The famous Firehole, at least in the geyser-basin stretches, is very spring creekish, and so is the Gibbon in the high meadow section above the falls.

The most wonderful aspect of spring creeks is their consistency. They always have just about the same flows, and water temperatures are amazingly constant in all seasons. This is an ideal situation for trout and aquatic insects, both of which thrive in such an environment. Western spring creeks can be fished in all but the worst winter weather. I once did quite well on Armstrong in a heavy snowfall. And rainstorms, which cause freestone streams to flood and muddy up, have little effect on spring creeks.

Spring creeks also have a hospitable chemistry, as they tend to be rather alkaline. This accounts in part for the rich plant growth that most of them have in abundance: watercress, elodea, mint along the banks. Instream vegetation supports an enormous population of insects and crustaceans. Some, such as the shrimp and the scud, are of no direct value to the dry-fly fisher. However, they cause trout to grow quickly to great size and vigor, and enable these small streams to hold an unbelievable number of large fish.

My friend Dr. Ray Najem has just fooled an emerger-eater in very tough, flat water on DePuy's Spring Creek. Not bad work for a guy from Ohio!

INSECT LIFE

There are exceptions, but most spring creeks do not have a wide variety of aquatic insects. This is compensated for by the great bounty of those species they do have. For example, the Pale Morning Duns start coming on western spring creeks in mid-to-late June, and are still hatching well into August. The sulphur hatch (*Centroptilum*) may last nearly as long. And diptera in incredible numbers are present at all times. These insects account for the superb off-season fishing spring creeks offer.

A few spring creeks do have hatches of large mayflies. I know of one in particular that has *Drunella grandis*, the western green drake, in quantity. But typically, the insects found in spring creeks are small. I cannot recall ever having seen a mayfly or caddis on the Paradise Valley streams larger than a #16. Stoneflies are practically nonexistent.

Terrestrial insects are usually very plentiful around such creeks, because of the terrain. Spring creeks do not suffer from low, warm water in summer, so terrestrial fishing is usually excellent. The trout seem to have a great yen for these insects. I recall many spring-creek afternoons when I did much better with an ant or beetle than with an imitation of the hatch fly that was emerging.

Some western spring creeks have damselflies in the wide, slow pools. Look for them on lily pads in quiet backwaters. Damselflies are primarily lake and pond insects, and they will come in for further discussion in that chapter, but keep your eyes open for them on the spring creeks.

Most people who fish spring creeks only occasionally tend to be hatch-focused. That's what they read about in the magazines: this hatch, that hatch. What seems to get lost in the hatch mania is that these duns come from nymphs, which in turn come from eggs, which are deposited by spinners. All too often, the imago is overlooked.

A case in point. In 1988 I spent a fair amount of time on the spring creeks. One long midsummer day was particularly unproductive. From two o'clock to around seven, I caught perhaps three small trout, and I worked hard for them. By then, everyone had gotten disgusted and had left. I had a similar inclination, but hesitated; how often would I have Armstrong's all to myself?

As I sat and watched the dormant stream, I happened to cast a glance over my shoulder. Hovering over a little irrigation ditch was a swarm of spinners, a silver cloud in the setting sun. My heart began to beat faster, and I prayed that these insects would soon appear over the creek. They did, and I am embarrassed to tell of the fishing I had in the following hour. If there had been a way to call back those disappointed anglers who had left early, I'd have done it.

A great thing about spring creeks is that they can be fished effectively year-round. Another Ohioan, Dr. Bob Dodge, with a rainbow from snow-lined Armstrong Spring Creek in late autumn.

Water Types

The relative flatness of the surrounding terrain disposes spring creeks to have more moderate variations in currents than do freestone streams. Some, in fact, are nothing more than deep ditches with slowly writhing currents; these can be mean and miserable. In such creeks, much of the fishing has to be done from land, because the banks drop off immediately and the bottom is virtual quicksand. The Letort is a prime example.

Other spring creeks feature riffle sections and stretches of moving water with a bit more character. The bottom is substantial enough that one can wade. Even so, structure is conservative: no boulders, rocks or pockets. In many cases, the vegetation provides most of the structure, offering deflections where trout can and do hold. There is a lot of this in the Firehole and the Henry's Fork, another spring-creek like freestone stream.

In the absence of rises, spring creeks can be tough to read, because the structure is inconspicuous—but, it *is* there. Casting to rises is much preferred, yet one can often do well on a spring creek by probing and prospecting, usually with a terrestrial.

In many cases one can spot individual trout in a spring creek, something that is less common in freestone streams. This is a definite plus, as it always helps to have a target. In streams where the trout are used to seeing people—the rod-fee streams are typical—they will often tolerate repetitive casts with the angler in full view, and vice versa. As we can observe the reactions of the trout to the fly, this can be most interesting.

Approach, Positioning, Presentation

First, I must tell you that the trout in spring creeks differ dramatically from stream to stream. This has everything to do with their familiarity with people. The rod-fee spring creeks and the public streams that get a lot of traffic fish altogether differently than do the private spring creeks where the fish exist in a wild and untrammeled state.

Trout do get used to people. I see this on all kinds of water, and particularly on spring creeks, which are comparatively small and intimate. I've waded across rod-fee creeks like Armstrong's and by the time I had reached the far bank, I'd look back and see trout starting to rise where I had walked moments before. These fish are what you call "acclimated."

Then there's the other extreme. Some western ranchers are generous enough to allow an angler or two onto their posted spring creeks now and then. These streams are quite small and the trout see few people. The fish are wild, streamborn, and unmolested; they eventually die of old age, or whatever natural calamity might befall them.

And talk about tough! Unless there is a lot of cloud cover, the least movement sends them streaking: the flash of a fly line in the air, the movement of a rod, an angler peeking over the bank, heavy footsteps. And I haven't even mentioned a cast falling onto the water!

This type of stream is not only an interesting challenge, it's an ideal training ground for the angler who wants to become truly proficient at taking trout on a dry fly under the most unforgiving conditions. Learn to fish here and you can fish anywhere. It can be done. What's required are patience and practice.

To be successful on the rod-fee creeks and well-travelled public streams—Idaho's Silver Creek, for example—one needs little more than the tools and techniques covered heretofore: the methods of approach and positioning, types of casts, drift management techniques and so forth. I will say that spring creek trout are usually very difficult to take casting up-and-over; they know about leaders. Across, across-and-down or downstream presentations are more effective. If the situation demands fishing upstream, try to get a good angle on the fish.

Tackle considerations are very important, especially regarding leaders and tippets. Also, you will want to learn as much local entomology as possible. Find out all you can about the insects you'll expect to encounter, both aquatic and terrestrial. And you will want flies that are designed for this type of fishing.

Commercial dry flies are often too heavily dressed for spring-creek fishing. Gentle currents and clear water call for sparseness and a clean silhouette, which accounts for the success of no-hackles, cut-wing thorax flies and such. Standard dressings may be satisfactory when a hatch is in full swing and fishing is relatively easy, but often a specialty style is more effective.

One of the problems the average fly fisher encounters on these streams is that the trout see the same flies every day. People buy their flies from a shop in the area that specializes in those creeks. The flies are the right ones for matching the current hatches, and are probably well tied. But fish do get to recognize them, and they get better at it as a particular insect progresses through its seasonal cycle. A group of trout start seeing a Pale Morning Dun imitation in late June and a month later they are still watching the same damn fly float past, a thousand times a day. It's amazing we catch any at all.

I would recommend a little variety. I mentioned terrestrials. I might also suggest a few general patterns in the size range of the prevailing hatch. The Adams is always a good choice, or the Light Cahill or the Quill Gordon. Anything to break the monotony.

Those of us who tie have an advantage, in that we can innovate. I have enjoyed great success using variations of the hatch pattern; still imitative, but with different character. Thorax-style dry flies are not commonly available in shops, but they are easy enough to tie, and work wonderfully on spring creeks. Sometimes a small parachute dressing will turn things around, or a little hackle-winged comparadun, or a shuck-dragger of some sort. Like pitching baseball, you can't get by throwing the same pitch every time. Even Nolan Ryan had to use a curve or change-up now and then.

Back to those maddening little spring creeks mentioned earlier; what might work there? Probably the two most important ingredients in success—even more so than presentation, choice of fly, length of leader, fineness of tippet and all the rest—are stealth and patience. The only other factor of comparable importance—and this you cannot control—is weather. An overcast day with a little drizzle can make things *so* much easier. But sitting around waiting for all of the pieces in the puzzle to fall into place is like waiting for Godot; we go fishing when we can, as often as we can.

There are times when taking a few trout on one of those streams is like Marine basic training: crawling around, casting lying down, sitting or kneeling for what seems like an eternity. And then the cast drops a mite too heavily and you are back to square one. But as I said, success is attainable, and when it comes, how sweet it is!

On this sort of water everything has to count, and there's little margin for error. It's generally not feasible to do any prospecting or muddling around, casting at random, trying to find out what will work. Blind casting to nervous trout that aren't in their feeding lies is worse than useless. Most of these creeks have little in the way of bank side foliage, causing the trout to feel terrible naked.

The exception is when there is good holding water along the banks. Then, meticulous presentations of terrestrials or even general patterns sometimes produce, because these streams often hold at least as many trout as there is food for, and the fish are aggressively hungry. Given a fair chance, they'll eat. And they tend not to discriminate. During an emergence, they will be selective, as trout usually are when hatch-bonding occurs. Otherwise, they simply want food: cheeseburgers, chili dogs and fries. Proper service is the key.

I'll always remember this incident. I had fished a pale morning dun hatch on a spring creek, with fair success. It was over; except for an occasional ring on the surface, all was quiet. I rose from my sitting position against a bank and happening to look upstream, saw that several trout were still out in their feeding positions. Like Oliver Twist, they wanted more!

The one nearest the bank was a beauty. I tied on a #12 Adams Parachute and cast upstream about a foot to the fish's streamward side, hoping not to alarm the creature. The fly landed nicely, was immediately attacked, and I blew it; in my excitement, I struck much harder than necessary and broke off. The trout, a red-spotted brown of at least four pounds, made a U-turn and swam downstream, passing within a few feet of where I knelt, chewing purposefully on the alien presence in its jaw. What could I say? At least I hooked the fish, and one out of two ain't bad.

But the best time is hatch time, and it's most beneficial to have a pretty good idea when that will be. Show up early, choose your spot, hunker down and wait it out. This requires patience. It helps to have a thermos of coffee along, and perhaps a book.

The author with a bank-feeding brown that made a rare mistake on a size 22 Sulphur.

On my first encounter with such a creek, I thought it best, when presenting to rising trout, to get upstream of them, keeping a low silhouette and making downstream drifts. Wrong! I soon learned that the trout could see line and rod movement from such a great distance that it was infeasible to attempt such a presentation. The least mud or debris scuffled up off the streambed would also put the fish down. There may be situations where the layout of the stream allows such a technique, but only with some cover, such as a background of foliage, to camouflage casting movements, and a place to stand without disturbing the streambed. I also think it would have to be a dark day.

So it's usually up-and-over, and make the best of it. You will want a shorter rod, seven-and-a-half or eight feet, and the longest leader you can effectively manage. For me, that's twelve to fourteen feet, depending on wind and casting range. I can lay out a longer leader—sixteen to eighteen feet—if the casting range is such that I can get plenty of line moving rapidly through the air, generating lots of impetus. But on these small streams the cast seldom exceeds thirty feet, and if about half of that is leader, you cannot effectively load the rod.

For those who prefer to make their own leaders, I offer a formula that I find efficient for presenting small flies:

4.5 feet of .018 thousandths
2.0 feet of .015 thousandths
1.5 feet of .012 thousandths
1.0 feet of .009 thousandths
9 inches of .007 thousandths
A tippet of .005 or .004 thousandths

You can vary this formula to make the leader longer or shorter. I use Maxima down to the .009, then the new high-strength limp stuff. I use blood knots for all connections except tying on the tippet, to minimize bulk. An exception: if I'm going from the stiff type to the limp type material, I use a double surgeon's knot. For connecting the tippet, especially when dropping from. 007 to .004 (7X), I suggest the double-double surgeon's knot, which is simply a double surgeon's knot with the .004 doubled. This is an excellent knot for very fine material.

Still Waters

Lakes and ponds have long been considered the domain of the subsurface angler: the nympher, the streamer-troller, the sinking-line set. True, those methods are usually more productive, but on certain waters at certain times, the dry fly can be highly effective.

Lakes and ponds have hatches, spinner falls and invasions of terrestrials, just as streams and rivers do. Because a heavy river-and-stream focus pervades fly fishing literature, we do not have the finger-tip references to still-water insects that we have for stream insects. The scientific people have a lot of data, but little of it has been distilled into fly fisher jargon. John Merwin's excellent *Stillwater Trout* does contain a fair amount of dry-fly information.

In 1988 I was a guest at a private club in Adirondack pond country, and overheard the members talking about their forthcoming Hendrickson hatch. I told them, as tactfully as possible, that if they were referring to any of the three Ephemerellidae (subvaria, invaria, rotunda) that are commonly known as Hendricksons, there had to be some mistake, because they are all strictly moving-water species.

A couple of weeks later, I was sent a specimen in a bottle of preservative. It was pretty beat up. I showed it to one of our New York State biologists. He said he couldn't be absolutely certain, but he thought the insect to be *Ephemerella lutulenta*, based on descriptive material in a Cornell University paper. If that's accurate, and I think it is, that makes two lacustrine *Ephemerellidae* that I know of. The other is *E. lacustris*, a handsome blue-winged olive that is quite common on lakes and ponds in the Rockies.

On my 1987 trip to Labrador's Minipi region, I encountered huge mayflies hatching on the lakes. I believe they were *Litobrancha* (formerly *Hexagenia*) *recurvata*, but that's not a positive identification; there are several other possibilities, and perhaps more than one species was represented. All I can say is that when these winged frankfurters were on the water, the trout fed like crazy.

In 1985, I acquired a float tube, or belly boat, if you prefer, and found it to be absolutely wonderful for lake and pond fishing. I baptized it on Henry's Lake in Idaho, swimming damselfly nymphs around on a sink-tip line. To my astonishment, I found sizeable trout taking adult damsels on the surface around the lily pads. I had heard of this, but didn't believe it amounted to much. I was wrong. Next time out, I had damsel dry flies with me, and I haven't been without them since.

In 1988, Montana guide Al Gadoury and I fished a lake near Gardiner that has a heavy population of big rainbows. In the morning they took small nymphs, but later, as the speckled-wing *Callibaetis* duns began to pop out, they were vulnerable to the dry fly. We also had some good surface damselfly fishing that afternoon.

Later, on that same trip, Dave Corcoran of the River's Edge in Bozeman took me on a four-wheel-drive adventure to an alpine lake high in the Tobacco Root mountains. As we finned about in our tubes, a huge squadron of flying ants came zooming out over the water and the trout came boiling up after them. The topographical map told us we were at about 9200 feet. I had no idea ants lived in such elevations. It was a great way to find out.

Gulper fishing, as it is called, has become quite popular on various western lakes and reservoirs, such as Hebgen and Clark's Canyon. The name is derived from the gulping sound made by cruising trout as they takefloating insects. Hebgen has a good Trico hatch that gets the gulpers moving on calm mornings. This is a type of fishing I want to do a lot more of.

In addition to the ones already mentioned, several other forms of insect life can stimulate surface feeding. Caddis are not common in still water, but there are a few species that live there. One of them is huge and nocturnal. I've had them splat against the windshield at ten o'clock at night while I was driving beside a Montana lake. I've not had the opportunity to fish the hatch, but I'm told the trout rise to them with abandon.

Various Diptera also inhabit lakes and ponds in enormous numbers. This includes everything from small midges to large craneflies, the former being prolific in many waters. The Griffith Gnat in sizes 18 through 24 is a very useful fly when small midges are on the water. When craneflies are encountered, I resort to an improbable pattern called the Gangly Legs, a creation of my now-departed angling partner, Dud Soper. Tying instructions can be found in my book, *The Versatile Fly Tyer*.

Trout feeding along the edge of a pond.

Tackle and Accoutrements

Some sort of floating vehicle is a necessity for lake and pond fishing. I have mixed feelings about boats in trout water, motor boats in particular, but they certainly come in handy on larger lakes. I do think there should be restrictions on the size of the motor.

Boats can frighten fish, and sometimes prevent the fly fisher from getting within casting range. Enter the float tube. On my first tubing excursion, I was amazed at the tolerance of the trout toward my presence. During the hatch, I had trout rising so close that I was casting only the leader onto the water. Even the kicking required to move about didn't seem to bother the fish very much. Thus began my romance with the float tube.

Casting from a float tube is much easier with a long rod, at least nine feet. My current favorite is a nine-foot, six-inch graphite for a number six line; it gives me plenty of range and sufficient power to cast a dry damselfly, when required. A four- or five-weight is nice for fishing small flies. Contemporary graphite fiber makes such long, light rods practical.

I want to mention several important points concerning tubes. When you are out there in your belly boat, it is your life support system, so get a good one. Rubber deteriorates over time, so inspect the inner tube every year and replace it when it shows any sign of cracking. Store your tube away from daylight and freezing temperatures, as both wreak havoc with rubber.

A float tube should have a substantial back rest, or you'll become fatigued. It should also have plenty of pockets for fly boxes and stuff, and Velcro fasteners to hold the rod securely while changing flies, releasing fish and whatever.

Neoprene stocking-foot waders are ideal for tubing, offering both warmth and flexibility. Boot-foot waders are heavy, and the boots won't fit into most fins. The waders need to be armpit length, as one rides quite low in a float tube. Polypropylene long underwear provides warmth in very cold water.

The only thing I find bothersome about tubing is answering calls of nature. I like my coffee in the morning, and on hot days, a beer with lunch. Both are diuretics. Whenever I go tubing, I pick out a secluded spot along the shore that I can fin to in a hurry. There's a limit to how fast one can propel a float tube so anticipate.

I recently treated myself to a new belly boat, trade named the U-Boat. It is shaped like a horseshoe. This makes it infinitely easier to get in and out of. The U-Boat costs more than standard belly boats, because it requires a special bladder, rather than a plain old truck tube. Believe me, it's worth the difference; what a joy! I plan on spending many happy days in this device.

PRESENTATION

Unlike pickerel or pike, trout are almost always moving in still water, for purposes of respiration and feeding. The gulpers typify surface-feeding

Still-water trout tend to be hefty, like this Montana rainbow, who posed briefly and reluctantly on the dock before being sent home.

procedure; they move to a fly and suck it in. Thus it is of great advantage to be able to tell where a fish is headed, so as to have some idea of where to place your cast.

When bugs are on the water, trout tend to develop a rhythm: swim-and-gulp, swim-and-gulp. At such times the angler can determine the course of a fish and predict with fair accuracy where the next gulp will occur. From a good vantage point it is possible to see the fish, polarized glasses being most helpful in this regard. However, the fish may also see you, which makes standing up in a boat a discretionary practice. If the fish is out a ways—fifty feet, let's say—it's probably okay to stand up, but even that depends on circumstances.

Still-water dry flies are usually presented in just that manner; still. In the case of rising fish, we cast to the spot where we anticipate a trout will be looking for its next gulp, and simply let the fly sit. If no pattern of movement can be determined, the next best ploy is to cast to the edge of the rise form, or slightly beyond it. Don't cast to the center of the ring, for that's the one place the trout *won't* be.

If damselflies are about and rises are visible inshore and around lily pads, make like you're bass-bugging; throw the fly into the little spaces between the pads and let it sit. A shorter leader and heavier tippet are called for here, as dictated by the size of the fly and the strength required to drag an angry trout out of the weeds.

Does it make any sense to fish dry flies on still water when there are no trout rising? Sometimes. On a lake or very large pond, probably not. On a smaller pond, where the water isn't overly deep and the fish are accessible, it may be quite productive. Again, the standard technique is to lay the fly out there and let it sit, but now and then I've found that a tiny twitch will get an apathetic trout's attention. Tiny, I said; no dragging flies across the pond.

A final thought. When going dry-fly trouting on a pond or lake, don't leave your terrestrials at home, especially those winged ants. The more still-water fly fishing I do, the more I run into these bugs. They seem to be all over the world and it's hard to anticipate when they will appear. Late summer and early fall seem to be prime times, but I've encountered flying ants in the spring as well. Keep a selection of black ones and brown ones handy, in sizes 12 through 20.

12

Salmon On The Surface

BOTH ATLANTIC AND PACIFIC SALMON WILL SOMETIMES TAKE A DRY fly. In the case of the Atlantic strain, the ones on this side of the pond are much more inclined to take a floater than those of Iceland, Norway and the British Isles. If memory serves, the famous match between Lee Wulff and Jock Scott, where Lee fished nothing but dry flies, ended in a draw; one salmon apiece. Early indications are that the rivers of the Kola Peninsula in northwestern Russia offer excellent dry-fly fishing for Atlantic salmon.

A discussion of dry-fly fishing for Atlantic salmon often leads to one of those hairsplitting arguments about what is and isn't "pure" dry-fly technique. The purists say that the fly must drift in a detached manner, and not leave a wake. That's fine, but quite often, salmon want the fly to drag a bit. Some of the best contemporary salmon dry fly patterns are actually designed to be fished in that manner, notably the Bombers and Buck Bugs. I don't get caught up in ecclesiastical debates; if the fly floats and is taken on the surface, that's dry enough for me.

My first salmon trip took me to Iceland's Grimsa (pronounced Grimsow) river. I was told by Toby, my ghillie, to forget about dry fly fishing; it simply didn't work there. He was quite right, as regards detached-drift fishing. However, I had in my box a couple of Bombers that Matty Vinciguerra had given me. I tried one in a stretch of broken water that the natives called Strengur: "strong currents." It accounted for two salmon and several heart-stopping swirls. The trick was to let it drag cross current just a little. Pure, maybe not; fun, most assuredly.

The Atlantic salmon; my biggest dry fly thrill.

FLIES

Salmon don't eat during their fresh-water migrations, so insect imitation is not a consideration, as an examination of any wet-fly salmon angler's fly box will attest. There are just a few patterns and styles of dry fly that consistently produce; Wulffs, Bombers, Buck Bugs and Irresistibles are about all one needs. The Royal Trude might make a good salmon dry fly, but I've never thought to try it.

In my opinion, pattern is subordinate to size and style of dressing. Most salmon drys found in fly shops are huge, and sometimes that's just the ticket. However, I've learned from the regulars on the Miramichi and its tributaries that a smaller fly often works better; Wulffs in size ten or twelve, and in low water, even fourteen. Whatever the size, the hooks must be strong, as even grilse will straighten or break a standard trout hook. This implies a rather generous dressing, as it takes a fair amount of hair and hackle to float such a hook.

Two bomber-style Atlantic salmon dry flies.

The Wilson salmon dry-fly hook made by Partridge of England is considered classic. They are a bit pricey, but then, how many salmon dry flies will the average angler go through in a lifetime? Be aware that these hooks conform to a different scale, and a size ten Wilson is considerably larger than a regular size ten dry fly hook.

The Wilson isn't the only hook on the market that can be used for salmon dry flies. Daiichi's model 2421 is a very good choice, and is stronger than the Wilson. Mustad offers a model 90240 that will serve the purpose, and is especially nice for Bombers, due to its slightly longer shank. The Partridge model N, which is actually a low-water wet fly hook, can be pressed into service for dries where more strength is desired; count on lots of hackle and a body with good floating properties. The same holds true for the Partridge model CS2SH, a turned-down-eye hook also known as the SEB. There are also several ordinary wet fly and nymph hooks that are quite adequate. They don't have to be black, that's essentially a style and tradition thing.

TACKLE

I've been criticized by the locals on just about every salmon river I've fished for using too light an outfit. So far, that hasn't hurt me, but perhaps the day will come. It's not that I advocate being under-gunned, I simply don't care for heavy tackle, and use the lightest that I find adequate for the job.

I feel that the weight classification of an outfit should be relative to the task at hand. An eight-and-a half or nine-foot seven- or eight-weight rod with a weight-forward line will cast practically any salmon dry fly a long ways with no problem. Given a proper reel and adequate backing, it will also facilitate playing and landing salmon from grilse size up to twenty pounds and more.

The type of water being fished has a bearing on tackle choice. In Iceland we encountered everything from very slow, meandering stretches to the powerful currents of Strengur. In the placid water, I am sure I could have landed a typical Grimsa salmon on a five- or six-weight. In Strengur, an eight- or nine-weight was advisable.

In rivers like the Restigouche, where some really huge salmon are found, I would definitely suggest a nine- or ten-weight, nine to ten feet in length, preferably with a short fighting butt. Some anglers use double-handed rods on such large rivers, which are an effective aid in casting, as well as playing salmon, especially when fishing from a boat.

The reel gets much more involved in fighting the fish in salmon fishing. A good drag system is important, one that allows fine-tuned adjustment of tension. It should be constructed of heat-resistant materials, so that it won't seize up when a strong fish makes a long run. External rim control is a useful feature, although I wouldn't consider it mandatory. Multiplying reels offer the convenience of reeling in slack line in a hurry. The only problem with them that I am aware of is that they also multiply the effort required to play a fish with the reel. This is particularly notice-able in salt-water fly fishing. I do not feel this is serious with reels that have no greater than a 2:1 ratio.

A salmon reel should have plenty of capacity, as a generous amount of backing is advised. I prefer thirty-pound-test dacron or some other stretch-resistant material for backing on all large gamefish reels. For light salmon fishing for grilse and "two-salt" fish up to fifteen pounds or so, twenty-pound backing will suffice. Although I have yet to have a salmon get much more than a hundred yards into my backing, I load my reels with two hundred, and I look forward to the day when I'll need all of it!

My main concern regarding salmon leaders is that the material not be slippery or stretchy. The new high-pound-test-to-diameter materials are superb for most trout-fishing applications, but salmon are a different ball game; they often put enormous strain on a leader. Stretchy material does not have good knot strength or stability under heavy stress, and do not cast large flies at all well. I must advise that some of the knotless store-bought leaders are deficient in this respect. My favorite materials for heavy leaders at this writing are Maxima and Mason's. I use Maxima for tippets almost exclusively.

Salmon are not terribly leader-shy, and eight feet tapered to 2X usually provides adequate camouflage. However, in low water on bright days, the shadow cast by a leader will scare hell out of a salmon. In such cases, a leader of ten or eleven feet is called for, with a tippet of 3X or even 4X which, with today's improved monofilament, is practical for such work.

There are a number of complicated knots used for salmon and other large gamefish, and certainly they have merit. For tying a dry fly to a salmon leader, I'm completely satisfied with the tried-and-true improved clinch knot. The most important thing is to tie the knot properly and retie it after playing a fish, or after letting the outfit stand for a while, as knots tied in monofilament will loosen by themselves. The uni-knot is also a good one.

PRESENTATION

The most important factor in salmon fishing is knowing where there are salmon. The holding positions these fish prefer are selected purely on the basis of comfort; feeding has no bearing whatever. This makes reading salmon water somewhat different than reading trout water. Still, structure and current deflection are major determinants, as they are with trout.

There's no substitute for experience when it comes to locating salmon lies in a pool. Those of us who get a week a year on a salmon river obviously have problems developing this experience, unless we return to the same piece of water year after year and keep accurate records of what we encounter. This is where a competent guide can make all the difference. A salmon guide's main stock-in-trade is knowing his water. Fly selection runs a distant second.

When fishing a salmon river, we often see these magnificent fish leap from the water, shake their sleek, powerful bodies and fall back with a resounding splash. It's a powerful temptation to cast to these fish, but usually not a productive procedure. Leaping fish are generally not taking fish. Rolling, porpoising salmon are entirely another matter; fish that behave in this manner are prime candidates, and they have identified their locations to the angler.

Presenting a detached-drift dry fly to a salmon is the same as for a trout. Accuracy and precision are of prime importance. Lacking a feeding urge, salmon aren't inclined to move very far to take a fly. If it comes to them in a way that pleases them, perhaps the rise will follow.

Salmon take a dry fly quite differently than trout. Their rises are more deliberate—the larger the fish, the more so. Grilse may take a fly with a quick move, but true salmon, those that have reached ten pounds or more, are almost whale-like in their rise form.

The toughest thing for most salmon dry-fly fishers is to restrain the strike until late in the rise form, when the salmon is well into its downward movement. Striking prematurely will almost invariably result in hooking nothing but air. This is a problem the down-and-across, wet-fly fisher doesn't encounter, as the fish take on a tight line and hook themselves. Misses will occur, but usually it's the salmon that has missed, not the angler.

A missed strike may put a salmon down, but unless contact was made, this is not necessarily so; in fact, it may work just the other way. When a salmon has decided it wants to play, it can become quite insistent, and a missed fly can stimulate the urge to rise. It is good practice, after such an incident, to let the fish settle down for a couple of minutes, marking its location as accurately as possible.

The inexperienced salmon dry-fly fisher has a tendency to give up on a fish too soon. It's not like trout fishing, where a fish that wants to feed will usually take the first good presentation it sees. Persistence is the key to success. Sometimes it takes fifty or sixty passes over a salmon before drawing the slightest response. This may be no more than a changing of body attitude in the current, but it may have great portent.

After such a move, or perhaps an inspection rise with no strike, it is probably wise to switch flies. This could mean a different size, pattern, type, or all three. A good tactic is to go back at the fish in increments. Start with two feet less line and add to it six inches at a time. A salmon that has risen may slightly alter its position, and the moderate variations in casting distance may put the fly into the fish's new drift line. Unless frightened, a salmon that has moved to a fly will probably take sooner or later, even if only out of aggravation.

Earlier we mentioned a style of dry fly known as the Bomber. It is one of the best. Its dramatically different silhouette and behavior make it a great teaser, and a wonderful fly to use as a locator. It is also a good choice when a response has been obtained and it's time to switch patterns, in an effort to draw the strike.

The Bomber is ideal for that "impure" form of dry-fly salmon fishing, whereby the fly is induced to drag a bit, leaving a little wake on the surface. For this sort of presentation, position yourself upstream of the fish or holding lie, as though presenting a wet fly. Simply control the amount of drag, so that the fly skids crosscurrent just a little, and is slightly restrained. This technique was very effective in Strengur on the Grimsa, where the currents were perfect for it.

Except where water conditions make it impractical, dry-fly fishing can be a great way to locate salmon. It enables the angler to cover a lot of likely looking water with precision, making repetitive casts. When the rise comes, the salmon has shown itself; short of an actual hookup, this is the best thing that can happen to a salmon fly fisher. Having located the fish, the angler may now try for it with a different dry fly, and if that fails, a wet fly.

For reasons unknown, salmon take dry flies in some rivers far more willingly than in others. The technique has never found much favor on the eastern side of the Atlantic, except for certain rivers on Russia's Kola Peninsula. In Canada a number of rivers are noted for their dry fly fishing. These include some northerly ones, such as the Whale and the Eagle, and the marvelous Jupiter on Anticosti Island. The Miramichi system offers good sport to the floater in summer months, and features plenty of public water. At this writing, a guide is mandatory for nonresident anglers. They are not expensive and a good one is worth many times his pay. They do vary, so try to find out all you can through the outfitter who is setting up your trip.

PACIFIC SALMON

Little is written about dry-fly fishing for the five species that make up Family Oncorhynchus, the Pacific salmon indigenous to North America. It wasn't so many years ago that Pacific salmon were considered next to impossible to catch on flies of any sort, but that's all changed. Now, swarms of anglers journey to Alaska, British Columbia, Washington and Oregon in pursuit of sport.

As for the dry fly, I've had some success in Alaska, and I'm sure I would do really well if I could just hang in the right spot long enough. To date, my Alaska trips have all been in late season, because that's silver salmon (coho) time, and they are the most fly-oriented of the five species. I cannot speak from personal experience regarding the other four, but have been informed that fresh-run sockeyes will occasionally take a floating fly.

My first day of silver salmon fishing was very successful. We had the good fortune of intercepting a large school of fresh-run fish, and they were aggressive. In the afternoon, we came upon a quiet backwater and the guide asked if I would like to have a go at salmon on dries. I replied that I would love to, but the only dry flies I had were strictly trout flies tied on light-wire hooks.

"Didn't I see a few hair mice in your box?" he said.

Myself and guide with an Alaskan silver salmon, or coho. With jaws like that, a mouse pattern presents no problem.

A typical mouse pattern. This fly works well for bass, pike, pickerel and the large Labrador brook trout, which often feed on lemmings.

"Yes. Will they work?"

"If these fish want a fly, anything will work."

I rigged up a mouse and in accordance with the guide's instructions, cast it out onto the flat water and let it sit. The slow currents carried the fly in an elliptical drift. Suddenly there was an enormous boil beneath it. I struck, and came up empty.

"They like it!", said the guide. "Try again."

I did so, and this time, I connected. A bright fish cleared the water by a good five feet, shaking the fly like a terrier shakes a rat. This, I tell you, was some kind of exciting! I took three salmon in that pool and two more in the next one before the float plane came to take us in.

A take by a silver. Talk about a rise!

The last day of that trip provided a second opportunity for silver salmon dry fly fishing. I spent the morning playing around with two-to-five-pound rainbows, huge grayling and sea-run Dolly Vardens. At lunch, one of the guides said that he had found a pool full of silvers about a half-mile downstream, and would anyone like to try for them? I volunteered.

This setup was a little different. The pool was very slow, but it was a pool proper, not a backwater. As a warm-up, I caught a few salmon on wet flies, and then knotted on a large Royal Wulff I'd tied at the lodge. Dead-drifting the fly produced nothing, but when I inadvertently let it drag, a fish attacked it and was hooked. The technique worked quite well, and I got several more salmon in this manner before they tired of the game. I thought about my boxes of Bombers and Buck Bugs back home and wished I had brought a few along.

An Alaskan dry-fly bonus: the ubiquitous, eager, surface-conscious Arctic grayling.

A Few Tricks

As dry-fly fishing evolves and its technology develops, we are seeing some interesting innovations that contribute to our effectiveness in various ways. They take several forms: aids in presentation, better equipment and support systems, improved methods of doing things. I'd like to pass some of these along.

The Strike Indicator

Probably you are aware that strike indicators are a valuable implement in nymph fishing, but did you know they can be most helpful with the dry fly as well? Think of all those occasions when the light was such that you couldn't see your fly on the water. You weren't sure whether it was floating properly or dragging, and when a rise occurred, you couldn't tell whether or not it was to your fly. And of course, all of this is exacerbated when the fly must be very small.

The strike indicator neatly solves the location and visibility problem by serving as a marker buoy of sorts. There are several types. The one that best suits the dry fly is the yarn type. It is attached eighteen to twenty-four inches from the fly with a double surgeon's loop. It should be quite small and inconspicuous; trim with a small pair of scissors, such as those used in fly tying.

Dave Corcoran turned me on to the technique. We were on the Big Horn, fishing to midges in the morning and small Baetis in the afternoon. The light was mean, especially later in the day, that silvery reflection that obscures even good-sized flies. I was having a wicked time of it.

My first reaction when Dave suggested an indicator was negative—what about casting, delicacy of presentation, spooking the trout? He said to trust him, and rigged me up. I soon learned that my fears were groundless. There was little impedance to casting and no alarming splash when the indicator landed on the water. I immediately began to fish much more effectively, and have been in love with indicators ever since.

My preferred method of mounting a dry-fly indicator is to use a tippet of approximately twenty inches in length and attach the yarn to the section immediately preceding the tippet. For example, if I'm fishing 6X, the section adjoining the tippet will be 4X or perhaps 3X, which accommodates the knot much better than 6X. I make the double surgeon's loop, insert a short doubled-over piece of yarn, tighten, and trim. Refer to the illustrations for details.

Indicator yarn is available in most fly shops and catalogs. It comes wrapped on a card. A handy dispenser can be fashioned out of an empty film canister by cutting an "X" in the lid. Then simply remove the yarn from the card, stuff it into the canister and run the end out the cut.

Another convenient method for carrying indicator yarn is to cut it into one-inch lengths and put the pieces in a little plastic box. These can be pretreated, as the yarn needs some paste flotant to keep it on top. Apply it in conservative quantities, rolling the yarn between the fingers. Don't gunk it up too heavily, or there will be a negative effect on flotation. The best pastes I've found for this purpose so far are silicone Mucilin, Simms Fly Rise, and Gink. I'm sure there are others that are comparable. Don't use a liquid flotant.

Rigging up a dry-fly strike indicator. First, tie a double surgeon's loop knot in the leader 2 or 3 feet from the tip.

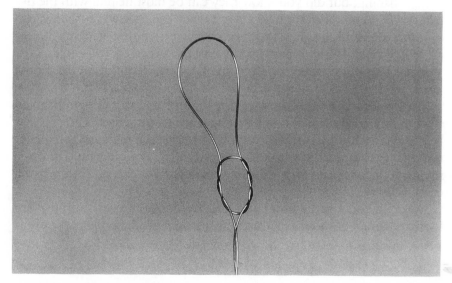

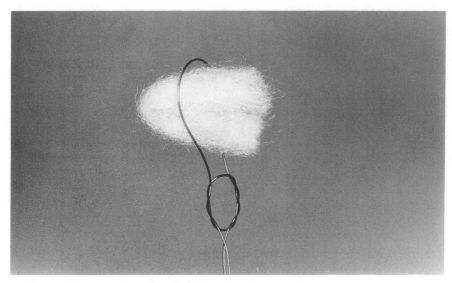

Insert a doubled-over piece of indicator yarn, as shown.

Pull the knot tight.

Trim to shape.

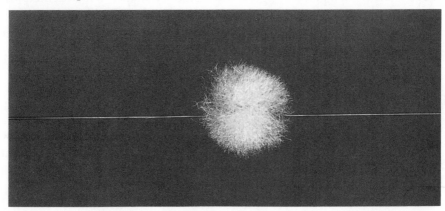

A handy rig for dispensing indicator yarn.

SCISSORS

A pair of fly tying or cuticle scissors comes in very handy in dry fly fishing. As mentioned, they are required for trimming indicator yarn; they also can be used to reconfigure a fly, trimming hackle and all sorts of things. I know; you hate the thought of having to hang one more implement on your fishing vest. So did I, but it was worth the small inconvenience.

A HAND WIPER

With success come problems; a trout is landed and must be handled. This inevitably means wet, slimy fingers, not the best for handling dry flies.

In an earlier chapter I mentioned that my solution is to carry a wiper. This consists of a piece of regular old-fashioned diaper that is secured just beneath the left arm hole of the vest with a safety pin. A small kitchen towel is also okay. After handling a trout, I rinse off the slime in the water and dry my hands on the cloth.

LEADER LOOPING

Anyone who has fished dry fly at all is aware that leader tippets must be changed quite frequently, for any one of a number of reasons. When light is failing and trout are rising like mad all over the place, fiddling with one's leader can be extremely frustrating.

Lefty Kreh passed this one along a number of years ago. I finally got around to trying it, and damned if it doesn't work! He suggests attaching tippet to leader with the interlocking-loop technique. One or several replacement tippets can be carried in little plastic envelopes, with loops in place. Thus, a tippet can be changed in short order. Lefty even goes so far as to tie on the fly he expects to be using and wrap a spare tippet around his hat, so that he can replace the tippet and fly in one simple operation.

Another technique involving loops is to attach a short section of butt material to the fly line with a needle or nail knot and make a loop in the end of it. This facilitates loop-to-loop connections involving the entire leader. It enables the angler to make radical changes in the leader quickly and easily, as conditions dictate. Ideally, the short permanent section should be of the same diameter as the butt section of the leader proper, or at least very close. In effect, the two function as one continuous section.

Fly Care

Well-tied flies are more durable than one would think, and can render long service, if properly cared for.

Thing number one, and I'm as neglectful in this respect as anyone, is to avoid mashing hackles on dry patches. It's best, when changing flies, to dry the one you're removing, perhaps with desiccant, and put it back in the box where it belongs. But if you must use a dry patch, I recommend the new ripple foam type. It holds a hook much more securely than lamb's wool, particularly a de-barbed hook. Also, the ridges are shaped in such a manner that dry-fly hackles can be kept out of contact with the patch, allowing them to dry in their proper position.

Thing number two: to take a moment to clear the eye after cutting off a fly. Use a stiletto to remove the old knot, which in all probability is stuck in the eye, and get any remnants of tippet material out of there. I can assure you that few things are more maddening than having to fool with this when the fish are slashing away and you want to put on a fly in a hurry.

Thing number three: don't overcrowd your fly boxes, jamming flies into the compartments until they resemble bird nests. Use boxes of adequate size for the flies they are to contain, and allow sufficient space that the hackles may deploy naturally.

Thing number four: after the season is over, remove the flies from their boxes and steam them. A jet from a regular tea kettle will do nicely. You can steam them in small groups in a little sieve, or individually, holding them with a hemostat. This will clean the flies and restore the hackles. Then they should be stored in a dry, uncrowded container with a few moth crystals.

And on that note, I wish you rising trout, hatches matched, dependable knots, and stiff hackles.

BIBLIOGRAPHY

CAUCCI, AL and NASTASI, BOB. *Hatches II*. New Jersey; Winchester Press, 1986. A comprehensive, yet practical treatise on stream insects for the fly fisher.

CLARKE, BRIAN and GODDARD, JOHN. *The Trout and the Fly*. New York; Lyons & Burford, 1980. An extremely well-researched, richly-illustrated work that provides a view of insects on the surface from the trout's angle.

FLICK, ART. *New Streamside Guide*. New York; Crown Publishers, Inc., 1969. A timeless, charming reference that introduces basic stream entomology to the newcomer.

HAFELE, RICK and HUGHES, DAVE. *The Complete Book of Western Hatches*. Oregon; Frank Amato Publications, 1981. A very fine angler's entomology, field guide and fly pattern reference for western hatches.

KREH, LEFTY. *Fly Casting With Lefty Kreh*. New York; J.P. Lippincott Company, 1974. A clear, easy-to-assimilate treatise on fly casting by one of its greatest exponents.

KRIEGER, MEL. *The Essence of Fly Casting*. California; Club Pacific, 1987. A wonderful book by the trainer of world champions, with the most beautiful photographs of casting ever.

LAFONTAINE, GARY. *Caddisflies*. New York; Lyons & Burford, 1981. A very important book, well-researched, generously-illustrated and beautifully written.

LEISER, ERIC and BOYLE, ROBERT. *Stoneflies for the Angler*. New York; Alfred A. Knopf, 1982. A excellent book on a little-understood subject by two of the finest angling writers of their time.

LIVELY, CHAUNCY. *Chauncy Lively's Flybox*. Pennsylvania; Stackpole Books, 1980. Perhaps the finest treatise on fly design ever written, by a master tyer and fly fisher.

MARINARO, VINCENT. *A Modern Dry Fly Code*. New York; Crown Publishers, Inc., 1970. Possibly the most original book ever written on the dry fly. Poetic, yet imminently practical.

MERWIN, JOHN. *Stillwater Trout*. New York; Lyons & Burford, 1980. An authoritative work on lake and pond trout fishing by one who knows it well.

SCHWIEBERT, ERNEST. *Matching The Hatch*. New York; MacMillan, 1955. A break-through book by a true fly fishing genius, still "must" reading after over thirty-five years.

SWISHER, DOUG and RICHARDS, CARL. *Selective Trout*. New York; Crown Publishers, Inc., 1971. A very important work on fly designs and trout's reaction to them.

TALLEUR, DICK. *Fly Fishing For Trout*. New Jersey; New Win Publishers, 1987. A comprehensive work on all aspects of fly fishing.

TALLEUR, DICK. *The Versatile Fly Tyer*. New York; Lyons & Burford, 1990. A detailed fly tying book, with much information for the dry fly fisher.

WULFF, JOAN. *Joan Wulff's Fly Casting Techniques*. New York; Lyons & Burford, 1987. One of fly fishing's greatest casters and instructors shows us how it should be done.

WULFF, LEE. *The Atlantic Salmon*. New York; A.S. Barnes, 1958. Beautifully written by arguably the greatest all-around fly fisher in history, and the ultimate authority on Atlantic salmon.

Index